MELTDOWN!

A Book of Real Solutions to Real Problems

Second, Revised Edition

Also by Paul D. Lunde

Great Restraint

Roosevelt's War

MELTDOWN!

A Book of Real Solutions to Real Problems

Second, Revised Edition

Paul D. Lunde

iUniverse, Inc.

Bloomington

MELTDOWN!

A Book of Real Solutions to Real Problems

Second, Revised Edition

Printed in the United States of America.

ISBN: 978-1-4759-8285-5 (sc)
ISBN: 978-1-4759-8286-2 (ebk)

iUniverse rev. date: 05/21/2013

This book is a work of nonfiction.

iUniverse books may be ordered through
booksellers
or by contacting:

iUniverse
1663 Liberty Drive
Bloomington, IN 47403 USA
www.iuniverse.com
1-800-Authors (1-800-288-4677)

Photographs by the Author.

Cover Photo

These giant wind turbines were photographed near the town of Blairsburg, Iowa. They are owned by an electric utility company. Wind turbines like these have become a common sight, in rural Iowa and in other parts of the country, in recent years. The electricity they produce is really a form of solar power, because the winds that spin the turbine blades are caused by the sun, heating and stirring our atmosphere, making the winds blow. Wind turbines like these could generate the electricity needed to separate water into its two components, hydrogen and oxygen. Hydrogen produced from water is free from carbon and therefore does not pollute the atmosphere. Hydrogen from water can make us truly energy independent, as described in the last article in this book, "The Truth About Energy Independence." Hydrogen from water has been called the "Forever Fuel" because we can produce an unlimited supply of it, right here in the U. S., and we will never run out of it. That's because water recycles. "Burning" hydrogen in our cars will not destroy it; the hydrogen combines with oxygen to become water again, and eventually falls back on the earth in the form of rain or snow.

For a bright future—with Karen, Thomas,
Erin, and Marie!

CONTENTS

INTRODUCTION TO THE SECOND, REVISED EDITION

I completed the first edition of *MELTDOWN!* in 2008, before the presidential election of that year. The Democratic candidate, Barack Obama, won the election, and we have since been subjected to his solutions to some of the problems that I wrote about in the first edition of this book, in particular the one I wrote about in Chapter Two therein, the one I called "Health Insurance? or Medical Care?"

His solution, called the Affordable Care Act (ACA) or, as the Republicans called it, Obamacare, was passed by Congress without a single Republican vote in either the House or the Senate. It was subjected to massive opposition in the Federal Courts, culminating in a decision by the U. S. Supreme Court, led by a 5-4 opinion for the Court delivered, in June, 2012, by Chief

Justice John Roberts, which upheld the constitutionality of the ACA but did not quiet Republican opposition to the ACA. Republicans, for the most part, vowed to repeal the whole thing. I took the position that *selective repeal* was the answer. I said, in a Letter to the Editor of the Des Moines *Register,* that only the mandates compelling purchase of Health Insurance should be repealed, because the ACA included some good features that should *not* be repealed. However, the apparent Republican candidate for president plunged ahead, promising to repeal Obamacare. Mitt Romney, himself, could not do it; Congress would have to vote on it. (It often irks me that candidates for president seem to think they are running for king, rather than the more limited office of President of the United States, but they almost all do it.)

Mitt Romney, of course, lost the election of 2012, and with it his announced intention of getting rid of Obamacare "on [his] first day in office." Romney also lost his pledge to do something about the "crushing debt" that he felt was burdening the American people. He would not be able to do anything about his promise to "create 12 million new jobs," or his proposal to make "North America energy independent by the end of his second term of office."

I wrote another Letter to the Editor of the Des Moines *Register* about that particular proposal, noting that Romney was running for President of the United States and not for president of North America (including Canada), but as far as I know, the *Register* never published that letter.

From what I have said here, you may get the impression that I was not a whole lot impressed by Mitt Romney's campaign pledges, even though I plead guilty to being a Republican, and you would be right. I had furnished copies of my original book titled MELTDOWN! to John McCain, when he was running for President in 2008, but I did not bother to do so in Romney's case, because it was obvious that his ideas on what to do did not include mine.

Romney and his unfortunate choice for running mate, Representative Paul Ryan, were proposing tax cuts and budget cutting that I saw as destructive to Social Security and Medicare, programs that are vital to the well-being of millions of Americans who have paid into those programs and reasonably expect them to be there, when they are needed by their Senior Citizen beneficiaries. The Romney/Ryan threat, for example, to turn Medicare into a voucher, ignored the reality that many Seniors would be unable to pay the difference and would thereby lose their vital health insurance protection. Romney and Ryan were making vague promises that they would not voucherize Medicare, but I did not trust them, particularly in light of what Ryan had already proposed, in the House, and another candidate for President, Newt Gingrich, had denounced as "social engineering."

I want to now depart from the 2012 election, and get on with my revised and expanded version of *Meltdown!* Months before the 2012 election, I had decided to publish this expanded version shortly after the election was history. The new version would be in three parts or sections. The first section would propose a second Bill of Rights for the nation.

The original Bill of Rights, the first ten amendments to the U. S. Constitution, had come about, mainly, because of what had happened during the ratification process. The group of men who drafted the Constitution during the spring and summer of 1787 had thought the document proposed a government that would be so limited in its powers that no Bill of Rights would be necessary. By the following summer, eight of the original 13 states had ratified the Constitution, and only one more was needed to bring it into effect. However, when the Virginia ratification convention assembled, it became immediately obvious that the Constitution had hit a stone wall.

Before the Virginia convention, there had been some objections to the Constitution as drafted, particularly because it lacked a Bill of Rights. Up to that point, it had been possible for Constitution proponents to get around the objections. But the Virgina convention was qualitatively different. A very distinguished group of Virginians had played the major role in getting the new Constitution this far. But an equally distinguished group of Virginians, led by the redoubtable Patrick Henry, now stood in opposition to ratification, their principal stated objection being the absence of a Bill of Rights. Virginia's State Constitution importantly featured a Bill of Rights, and Patrick Henry strenuously opposed the new Federal Constitution, ostensibly because it lacked a Bill of Rights. There lurked behind their stated objections something of a more sinister nature. The opponents really wanted no Federal Constitution at all, but that was an objection that the opponents did not want to admit to.

James Madison, faced with a situtation that might cause the entire ratification drive to unravel, publicly promised the Virginia opponents that he would see to it that a Bill of Rights would be added to the new Federal Constitution once the new government got under way. Madison's solution proved acceptable to enough of the delegates that Virginia's ratification was narrowly secured. Meanwhile, New Hampshire had voted to ratify while Virginia was still thinking about it, so the new Federal Consitution was now in effect, there being the minimally necessary nine States. Virginia made ten, and New York then voted to join the union, allowing the new government to start operations with eleven of the original 13 States aboard. (North Carolina and Rhode Island eventually joined, making it unanimous.)

Madison was elected to the House of Representatives, and as he had promised, he worked for adoption of a Bill of Rights. The notion that

Madison actually drafted the Bill of Rights is really a myth. Days of debate took place in both the House and the Senate, numerous ideas were presented, and what finally emerged was twelve proposed amendments to the U. S. Constitution. Numbers three through 12 were ratified by December of 1791. (Of the two that were not ratified at that time, one was finally ratified more than 200 years later and became what we know as the 27th Amendment; the other one became obsolete with the passage of time.) For more about this, see my notes in the Epilogue of this book.

In Section One of this book, I'm proposing twelve draft amendments, some of which are functionally similar to those in the original Bill of Rights. I'm hoping to get all 12 adopted at the same time, a tall order, I know. But all 12 are important, and I'm going to present all 12 of them, one by one, together with an explanatory article in each case. In Section Two, I'm proposing five additional draft amendments, for purposes of discussion. In Section Three, I'm including ideas for consideration by various levels of government—federal, state, and local or regional.

Some of these ideas have been presented before, either in the first edition of this book, *Meltdown!* or in correspondence with various government officials, such as members of congress. And some of these ideas are new ideas that I have written up but have never proposed previously to anyone. Some of these ideas may seem "far out," such as my proposal for new airports with 50,000-foot main runways. But I respectfully submit that all of these are good ideas and are actually not "far out" at all.

So here goes, starting with Section One, my proposals for 12 new amendments to the U. S. Constitution, all of which are needed *NOW,* as soon as they can be officially "proposed" by Congress and then ratified by the legislatures of three-fourths (38) of the "several States." I hereby invite **any** member of the U. S. House of Representatives, and **any** member of the U. S. Senate, to introduce any, or preferably, **all**, of these proposed amendments.

By the way, just a word about my qualifications for making these proposals. I have four earned college degrees, but the one most relevant here is a J.D. (Juris Doctor) degree from Harvard Law School, awarded in 1961. Not to brag, but my degree from Harvard Law School makes me one of the elite among the nation's lawyers. A couple of facts worth noting: 1) For the first time in history, both of the major candidates for President of the United States in 2012 were graduates of Harvard Law School, and I graduated from Harvard Law School before they did, so that makes me more experienced, as a lawyer, than either of them. 2) Five of the nine current members of the United States Supreme Court are graduates of Harvard Law School, and a sixth (Justice Ginsberg) attended Harvard Law School but wound up getting her law degree at Columbia. One of the current members, Mr. Justice Kennedy, is a classmate of mine at Harvard Law School and no, I have never met him.

None of the men who drafted the original Constitution, and none of the men who drafted the Bill of Rights, had ever even attended law school. That's because there had never been a law school, in the United States, at that time. I had the privilege, not only of graduating from Harvard Law School, but also of studying constitutional law there under the late Mark deWolfe Howe (I also took his course in

Admiralty Law, which is a special branch of Federal law).

And I have written two published books on the subject of the U. S. Constitution, *Great Restraint,* which was a how-to book on amending the U. S. Constitution via the convention method, and the one you are reading now, which is the revised and expanded version of *Meltdown!* I was admitted to the practice of law in the State of Iowa in 1961 (on the very day that I graduated from Harvard Law School), I was admitted to practice before the U. S. Supreme Court in 1964, and I served three years on active duty as an officer in the U. S. Army's Judge Advocate Generals Corps. Beyond these qualifications, I'll let you judge my amendment proposals for yourself. What I'm saying is that I am as qualified as anyone to draft proposals for amending the U. S. Constitution, so you're invited to take a look at them, and let's see what you think.

SECTION ONE

The Twelve Proposed (draft) Amendments [The Second Bill of Rights]

NUMBER ONE:

CHOOSING THE ELECTORS

The Electors chosen in each State shall be chosen in the following manner:

1. Those chosen in equal number to the whole number of representatives to which the State may be entitled in the Congress shall be chosen by the

popular vote of those adult citizens eligible to vote for each representative.

2. Those chosen in equal number to the whole number of senators to which the State may be entitled shall be chosen by the popular vote of those adult citizens eligible to vote for senator in each State.

3. Those chosen in the District constituting the seat of Government of the United States shall be chosen by the popular vote of the adult citizens thereof who are eligible to vote therein.

Preventing a Meltdown, Through Electoral Reform

We have a choice. The choice is between waiting for an electoral disaster to occur, and taking action now, to head off such a disaster.

The nature of the disaster I'm talking about would be a presidential election with the winning candidate being chosen by a majority of the Electors, with the losing candidate having received a huge margin, several *million* votes, in the popular vote. This result is likely to lead to a very substantial public demand to scrap the electoral system altogether. In other words, the *meltdown* I'm talking about here would be a meltdown of public support for the peculiar electoral vote system set forth in the United States Constitution, written in 1787 and little changed since.

Such a disaster almost happened, in 2004. Republican President George Bush, running for re-election, received a popular vote total of nearly 3 million votes (actually, 2,978,127) more than the vote for his Democratic rival, John Kerry. Bush's electoral vote total was 286, versus 251 for Kerry. In 2004, Bush's electoral vote margin came entirely from the 20 electoral votes he received from the State of Ohio. If Kerry had received the Ohio electoral votes instead of Bush, it would have been 266 for Bush, 271 for Kerry.

In Ohio, the Republican president had received a popular vote total of 2,859,764 versus 2,741,165 for his Democratic rival, Kerry, a margin of 118,599 votes. A shift of less than 60,000 popular votes *in Ohio* would have given the nod to Kerry in the electoral vote, the vote that mattered, even though Bush had nearly 3 million more popular votes nationwide, as set forth above.

This would not have been the first time in American history that the winner of the popular vote failed to win in the electoral vote. Indeed, President Bush himself had won the electoral vote in the 2000 election, with 271 electoral votes, while the loser, Al Gore had 266 electoral votes and a 530,893 margin in the popular vote.

Again, the results were entirely dependent upon who received the electoral vote in one particular state, in that case, Florida. The winner of Florida's 25 electoral votes had depended upon a 537-vote popular vote margin in Florida that Bush was finally declared to have received. In the 2000 election, it took a U. S. Supreme Court decision to finally put a stop to the efforts by Florida Democrats, some of whom were members of the Florida Supreme Court, to contravene state election laws in an effort to "recount" some of the ballots there in order to somehow "find" enough popular votes so that Gore, not Bush, would be the recipient of Florida's 25 electoral votes.

Many people, today, think the system of choosing Electors, who will in turn choose the president and vice-president of the United States, is out of date and should be scrapped altogether. However, that would not be easy to accomplish; it would require very extensive amendment of the U. S. Constitution, and it would involve a very extensive rethinking of our entire system of government. What I am going to do, here, is explain the electoral system itself, and then I am going to propose some relatively simple changes that will improve the electoral system without scrapping the features that the Framers of the U. S. Constitution intended as the very foundation of our system of government.

The U. S. Constitution was written by a large committee that met in the city of Philadelphia in the late spring and the summer of 1787. At that time, the 13 states encompassed a contiguous geographical area stretching along the east coast of the United States, from New Hampshire in the north to Georgia in the south. The fastest form of communication was by sea, but whether overland or by sea, it required a period best measured by days and weeks, at the quickest. The invention of the telegraph was decades in the future and could not have even been imagined by the delegates to what became known as the Constitutional Convention. Consequently, they had to work within the communication confines with which they themselves were familiar. The system of Electors was their solution to the communication problems of their time.

The delegates decided upon an executive that would be one person with power to act independently. The nature of the executive had been debated all summer and came about through many hours of deliberation and many votes. The question of who would choose the executive had also been extensively debated, and the answer was that "the people" would choose, which you may find hard to believe.

How would "the people" choose the president? How could they do so, given the communication problems prevalent in 1787, as set forth above? The solution which the delegates invented was really rather clever, when you stop to think about it.

In the Constitution as written in 1787, only the members of the House of Representatives were chosen, by "the people" from among the qualified "inhabitants" of each state. The qualifications included a minimum age of 25, residence within the state and U. S. citizenship for at least seven years. The voters were to be those persons eligible to vote for "the most numerous branch of the state legislature." The two senators from each state were chosen by the state legislatures, not by a direct vote of the people. (That, of course, was changed by the 17th Amendment to the U. S. Constitution, ratified in 1913.)

The delegates assumed that "the people" would know who to vote for when it came to choosing their own members of the U. S. House of Representatives. But how would "the people" know who to vote for, for president? This was the problem as the delegates saw it; "the people" would *not* know who to vote for! How could they, given the speed of communications prevalent at that time?

To solve this problem, *special* people, Electors, would be chosen from among "the people." The Electors were to be appointed "in such manner as the legislature . . . [of each state] may direct . . ." The number of Electors so appointed were to be "equal to the whole number of senators and representatives to which the state may be entitled in the Congress . . ." So, for example, since my state currently is entitled to four members in the U. S. House of Representatives, my state would get six Electors (including the two for my state's two senators). The Constitution says Electors can't, themselves, be senators or members of the U. S. House, nor is any other "person holding an office of trust or profit under the United States" eligible to be an Elector.

The Electors, chosen from among "the people" in each state, "shall meet in their respective states, and vote by ballot for two persons, of whom one at least shall not be an inhabitant of the same State with themselves." The Constitution says that "Congress may determine the time of choosing the electors, and the day on which they shall give their votes; which day shall be the same throughout the United States."

The Constitution, as originally written, spells out the voting procedure to be used by the Electors in choosing the president, and also the vice-president. That procedure worked all right when George Washington was the unanimous choice for president, as he was in 1788 and again four years later. It did *not* work when it came to choosing Thomas Jefferson for president. There was a tie, in the electoral vote for president, between Thomas Jefferson and Aaron Burr, who was supposed to be the choice for vice-president. The tie threw the election into the U. S. House of Representatives, and chaos ensued for a long while, with ballot after ballot taking place, and no choice emerging. Jefferson, fortunately, was the eventual choice for president, and Congress then proposed what became the 12th Amendment to the U. S. Constitution, ratified in the year

1804, which spelled out, in considerably greater detail, how the Electors would go about choosing the president and the vice-president.

I would here point out the fact that no substantial change in the speed of communication had taken place during the period between 1787 and 1804, so the rationale for using the electoral vote procedure still prevailed. The main procedural change made by the 12th Amendment stipulated that "distinct ballots" for president and vice-president were to be used by the Electors.

Obviously, it was intended that the persons chosen by the states to be Electors were to be knowledgeable people who would be aware of the people from whom the choice for president and vice-president would be made. So the Electors were to be chosen from among "the people" but they were *special* people, chosen as specified by the legislatures of the various states, which meant that the Electors would not necessarily be chosen in the same way in all of the states and, at least in the beginning, meant that they were not expected to be chosen by popular vote. That came later.

The big change came with the invention of the telegraph. Although the public demonstration of Samuel F. B. Morse's idea did not occur until 1844, there had already been efforts to relay messages from point to point by non-electronic means. Also, great improvements in transportation were taking place by the 1820s, with railroads coming on and with the Erie Canal's completion in 1825. With the vast improvements in both transportation and communication taking place early in the 19th century, there also came to be a public demand for a change in the way that Electors were chosen. Soon, the legislatures of all of the states opted for popular voting as the method for choosing Electors. The development of political parties brought in the idea of having lists of Electors supplied by the parties, with the voters choosing which slate (list) of Electors would then cast the electoral votes for that state. Thus was born the present system, prevalent in nearly all of the states, for choosing the Electors on a "winner take all" basis.

"Winner take all" in a state with a large population meant that all of the Electors from that state could be chosen by a bare majority of the population of that state. And thus a very large number of people in that state might find, in effect, that their votes for president and vice-president would count for nothing. If that happened in many states with large populations, the result could be that the president and vice-president are the choice of a majority of the Electors, but are not the popular vote choices overall.

As pointed out above, the 2000 Election saw George Bush elected president with a very small majority of the electoral votes (271 to 266, a five-vote edge) and with a majority of half a million popular votes going to the ***other*** major-party candidate (Al Gore). Now, add to that the further grief wherein Bush was declared the winner, by a very tiny margin (about 500 votes) in one state with 25 electoral votes, and with the United States Supreme Court having to overrule the Florida Supreme Court, which had partisan political connotations, and you had the ingredients for a disputed election which continues to echo.

And again, as described above, the 2004 Election was a near-disaster, going the other way, with Bush compiling a huge majority of the popular vote, winning that by nearly three *million* votes--

and almost losing the electoral vote to John Kerry. The edge for Bush in Ohio, which gave Bush 20 electoral votes and thus the election, looks decent, until you look into the nitty-gritty and find that there were widespread irregularities in the Ohio balloting that easily could have wiped out Bush's margin and sent that election into a tail-spin. On the Internet, I recently reread the very interesting article on the 2004 Election in *Rolling Stone*. If even a few of the voting irregularities described in that article were true, the results in Ohio very well could have been different.

And if Ohio had delivered its electoral vote to Kerry, the resulting *meltdown* that I described in the opening paragraphs of this article could very well have already occurred. No matter how you may feel about President Bush now, it was abundantly clear that he was the nation's choice, over Kerry, (then a U. S. Senator, now the Secretary of State,) in 2004. The degree of frustration that Bush's voters would have felt at that time, with their three million vote margin rejected in order to elect a president who was clearly the choice of only a minority of the people voting, using a voting procedure that would have been seen as two centuries obsolete, would have been overwhelming.

It is with the foregoing situation in mind that I now present a modest proposal for overhauling the electoral vote system quickly, and hoping thereby to save it from being tossed aside in haste as a result of what I term a *meltdown.* The key change proposed is to give the voters ***in each congressional district*** the right to choose ***their*** presidential Elector by popular vote. This changes the "winner take all" result in all states that have two, or more, members of the U. S. House of Representatives.

The Proposed Amendment that I showed you, above, is for an amendment to the U. S. Constitution that would preserve the positive aspects of the historic electoral vote system, and simply makes the electoral votes more representative of the underlying popular votes. Paragraph 1 says that the adult citizens who are eligible to vote for their member of the U. S. House of Representatives also would be eligible to vote for their presidential elector.

You will notice that I left the electoral votes for senator on a "winner take all" basis. I considered the idea of changing this but rejected it. There is just no good way of dividing this vote that can stand scrutiny, from a historical point of view. No matter what State you live in, you only choose your two senators one at a time, and in every third national election, you don't vote for senator at all.

The proposal I am making, here, is intended to preserve the traditional electoral vote system, which I think is worth preserving. The States of Maine and Nebraska already choose their electors by congressional district, so the amendment I am proposing, here, would have no effect on those two states. But in a big State like California, my proposed amendment would allow the Republicans who live in districts with a Republican majority to choose a Republican elector, while in Texas, Democrats who live in districts with a Democratic majority would be able to choose a Democratic elector. And thus, the electoral vote would more closely reflect the underlying popular vote.

The Founding Fathers never intended to make certain States "swing states" or "battleground states." They never intended that professional politicians would be able to "game" the electoral vote system, which is now increasingly the case. They never intended to effectively disenfranchise millions of voters in the nation's biggest states. But that has been the practical result, and it is time to make this change in our Constitution, by way of modernizing it, without throwing out the electoral vote system altogether.

President Barack Obama got 332 electoral votes in the 2012 election and had 51.1 percent of the popular vote, numbering 65.9 million. Mitt Romney, the Republican candidate, got 206 electoral votes from the 24 States he carried. His share of the popular vote was 47.2 percent, 60.9 million. Obama won 26 States and the District of Columbia, which by virtue of the 23rd Amendment gets three electoral votes but has no voting member in Congress and is not a State. You'll notice that my proposed amendment Number One has the electors from D. C. chosen at-large on a winner-take-all basis, as is presently the case. They are all three Democrats, and they always will be Democrats, as far as the eye can see, which explains why the Republicans will always block attempts to make D. C. a State, something that would add two senators, who would also be Democrats, forever.

You will also notice that 1.7 per cent of the total vote, about 2.2 million votes scattered across the country, went to various third-party candidates. They got no electoral votes at all, which is usually the case. Every presidential election year, there are always some people who foolishly talk about running for president as a candidate for some "third party." But the Constitution, in Article II, requires that the president must be the choice of the majority of the electors, which is 270 at the present time.

If no candidate for president gets a majority of the electors, the president is chosen by the vote of the members of the House of Representatives, where each State gets one vote. The Senate chooses the vice president. Only once, in U. S. history, has this nightmare scenario taken place, where the president is chosen by the House because of a tie in the electoral vote between what was then supposed to have been the candidates for president and vice president. It happened due to a drafting error by the Framers of the Constitution, which was promptly corrected by the Twelfth amendment, proposed by Congress in December of 1809 and ratified by the following July, amazingly fast considering the primitive means of communication that were still the fastest available at that time, decades before the invention of the telegraph.

The choice of Thomas Jefferson as president, over Aaron Burr, who was supposed to be the candidate for vice president, required many votes in the House. The last time there was a serious chance that neither of the major party candidates would get a majority of the electoral votes took place in 1992, the year that I happened to be a major party candidate for a seat in the U. S. House of Representatives. Ross Perot was spending millions of dollars running for president as a third party candidate, in a year that neither of the major party candidates was perceived to be a very strong contender. I gave some serious thought to the possibility that I might win my election, and have to participate in a House vote for president.

Perot did, in fact, seriously influence the vote for president, because he polled close to 20 per cent of the popular vote. It is possible that Perot got enough votes that would otherwise have gone to the Republican candidate (the first George Bush, who was seeking his second term) to prevent him from getting enough electoral votes for a majority; the winner was the Democratic candidate, Bill Clinton.

But despite his huge popular vote (vastly larger than most third party candidates achieve), Perot did not win a single electoral vote. From my perspective, Perot made no effort to help any candidate for Congress, who might have then helped him win the election if the House wound up having to make the choice. The fact that Perot, as a third party candidate, won millions of popular votes but not a single electoral vote, simply illustrates the fact that the U. S. presidential election system offers little real opportunity for any third party candidate to win.

At most, a third party candidate can siphon off enough votes to cause one of the two major party candidates to lose, as *may* have happened in 1992, but a third party candidate cannot actually *win* a U. S. presidential election. That's the reality behind any third party threat in a U. S. presidential election, and it can indeed threaten any major party candidate who is perceived by the voters as weak. Given the large field of Republicans who were seeking their party's nomination in 2012, Mitt Romney's candidacy could very well have been sunk if one of the more prominent ones had posed a serious third party threat. Indeed, there were a number of such threats that simply never materialized.

Romney himself may have made the vice presidential choice he did as a means of discouraging such a third party threat or at least major defections from within the Republican party itself. My perspective is that he doomed his own candidacy by his vice presidential choice, which lost him a lot of the Social Security/ Medicare vote, and threatened women with the very real possibility that he would curb their reproductive rights. Romney's foolish pledge that he would work for overturning the Supreme Court's *Roe v. Wade* abortion decision may very well have cost him the election.

TV commercials that showed him in a bad light on a number of major issues no doubt were important factors in Romney's loss of the 2012 election, which was definitely his to lose because the poor economy was a millstone around President Obama's neck. All Romney needed, to win, was 64 more electoral votes, which he could have had with only a few more popular votes in the "swing states" (given the winner-take-all policy in all of those states).

Obama's huge popular vote majority was mostly wasted in states like California and New York. The superior absentee vote efforts by the Democratic Party organization did pay off in states like mine (Iowa) where Romney actually won with the voters who came out on election day, but lost the many voters who felt threatened enough to have voted against him, in advance. For that is how Romney lost: the majority of the electorate voted *against* Romney, and Obama was the only other choice, even though many voters did not want Obama, either; Obama was seen, by many voters, as the lesser of two evils.

Well, so much for the 2012 election. I urge all of the members of Congress to work together to get this amendment passed, and ratified, before the 2016 presidential election, so that their constituents can actually have their votes for president count.

NUMBER TWO:

THE AMERICAN TRADITIONS

Notwithstanding the provisions of the First Article of Amendment, the continued use of the traditional words "In God We Trust" on coins and currency of the United States of America, and the continued use of such language in the public ceremonies of the United States and of the several States and of their political subdivisions, shall not be considered infringements of the Constitution. No celebrations of the traditional Christmas, nor those of other religious traditions, shall be banned pursuant to the First Amendment except to the extent they may raise a reasonable risk to the health of participants therein. No participation or attendance in such religious traditions or celebrations shall ever be required, but no such celebrations need be altered merely because some nonparticipants happen to be present, and nonparticipants shall always have the unobstructed right to leave any area where

such celebrations are taking place. The traditional use of the Bible, or other religious books, in public ceremonies, such as in those involved in the "swearing in" of public officials or jurors, shall never be banned. Public officials, jurors, and others shall always have the right to affirm the truthfulness of their undertakings if they do not wish to use the traditional wording of oaths or other affirmations, and no use of any religious book in any public ceremony shall ever be required by law.

No traditional legal system, other than that of the English common law, shall ever be recognized in any of the courts of the United States or in those of any of the several States, and no decision of any foreign court may ever be cited or relied on as precedent in the United States of America.

The American Traditions Amendment Proposal

This amendment proposal comes very close to being self-explanatory; just look at the text. In the years since World War II, traditions that older Americans took for granted have been increasingly under attack. Teachers have been forbidden to have their children sing Christmas carols by nervous administrators, fearful of law suits. The saying of a prayer in a high school graduation ceremony has been banned. At any time, the words "In God We Trust" on our coins and currency may be vanquished. The custom of using the Holy Bible during the swearing-in ceremony may suddenly become a thing of the past.

The Founding Fathers forbade an establishment of religion in the First Amendment, yet never dreamed that these very words might someday be turned against customs and traditions that they unquestioningly assumed.

The purpose of this draft amendment is to try to restore the customs and traditions that we Senior

Citizens grew up with, before they were attacked as violative of the First Amendment. I do not claim this draft is perfect, but I think it is a useful starting point and it is better than nothing. It is intended to restore the Christmas traditions that we knew as children, so that we can pass them along to our children and grandchildren. We are enriched by the traditions of others, and this amendment proposal is intended to protect them also.

The final provision is intended to protect our courts from efforts to import foreign legal traditions; the original source of our legal system was the English common law, and without it, this country would not be the country we know it to be, today.

NUMBER THREE:

THE BALANCE-THE-BUDGET CONSTITUTIONAL AMENDMENT

Section 1: The Congress shall have no power to borrow money, whether on the credit of the United States or otherwise, to finance current or future expenditures, except following a declaration of war, or following a declaration of great national emergency by the president.

Section 2: If the president shall declare a great national emergency, any senator or representative, within the ten days following such declaration, shall have the right to file a petition in the Supreme Court for the purpose of questioning the existence of such emergency. The Supreme Court, sitting as a court of original jurisdiction, shall promptly hear the evidence thereon presented by the parties and shall render its decision, based on proofs similar to those required in civil cases

generally, within the sixty days following such declaration.

Section 3: Nothing contained herein shall be construed to prevent the United States from borrowing money to the extent necessary to repay past debts as they come due, but such borrowing shall not be for the purpose of paying interest. The Congress shall not appropriate funds to retire such past debts in excess of ten per cent thereof, or one trillion dollars, whichever is greater, in any period of twelve consecutive months; except this shall not apply when the total of such past debts shall be less than one trillion dollars.

Section 4: The president shall send to Congress, at least annually, a budget showing proposed receipts and expenditures, which budget shall be in balance.

Section 5: If the Congress approves expenditures which exceed anticipated revenues for any period of twelve consecutive months, the president shall reduce the expenditures generally, or disapprove specific expenditures, in an amount sufficient to bring them into balance with anticipated revenues.

Section 6: The foregoing Sections 4 and 5 shall not apply following a declaration of war by the Congress, or following the declaration of a great national emergency by the president, until such time as such declarations are no longer in effect; and such declarations shall terminate three years from the date declared unless renewed by the president annually thereafter.

Section 7: For the purpose of balancing revenues and expenditures, the Congress shall have the power to levy a tax on sales of goods at retail, to the ultimate consumer, but the total revenues raised by such tax shall in no event exceed fifty per cent of total expenditures.

Section 8: The tax authorized by this Article shall not be levied against food for human consumption, sales or rentals of real estate, contracts of insurance approved for sale by the several States, and capital or debt instruments of the several States or of private companies. The Congress shall have the power to exempt from the tax additional categories of goods, and in no event shall this tax apply to goods fairly within the ambit of

the First Article of Amendment. The rate of such tax shall be adjusted not less often than annually.

Section 9: This Article shall become effective on the first day of January following its ratification.

How to Take Away the Congressional Credit Card

I hardly need to tell you that the U. S. Congress has been engaged in deficit spending for many years. You already know that. What you want to know is: How to put a stop to it? In this article, I'm going to give you the answer to that all-important question.

When they wrote our Constitution, in the summer of 1787, the delegates to the Philadelphia Convention included some very innocent-looking language that has cost all of us a ton of money in the years since. They meant well, of course, when they wrote that Congress shall have the power . . . To borrow money on the credit of the United States . That's all they said about borrowing money. Not a word about paying it back! This language is found in Article I, Section 8 of the U. S. Constitution, and not a word of it has ever been changed in the years since 1787.

For a long time, Congress used the power to borrow money on the credit of the United States very responsibly. Even when the borrowing was for purposes of fighting a war, Congress has always, until quite recent times, seen to it that the borrowed money was paid back, within a reasonable time. Example: During the Civil War era, Congress enacted a personal income tax to help pay for the war's very large expenses. That income tax ended in 1866. In 1880, the U.S. Supreme Court heard arguments challenging an income tax as an unconstitutional direct tax, but decided against that line of argument. Congress passed the Income Tax Act of 1894, expecting it to be approved by the Supreme Court. However, the Supreme Court, in 1895, reversed itself, deciding, 5-4, that the income tax was, indeed, a direct tax, not apportioned among the States and therefore, unconstitutional. The Supreme Court even reheard the case, but again, decided 5 to 4 against the income tax.

The 16th Amendment to the Constitution authorizing an income tax was proposed by Congress in 1909, and was ratified by the State legislatures in 1913, just in time for Congress to use the income tax to help finance World War I. By the end of the 1920s, thanks to the income tax, most of the World War I debt had been paid off.

But, just before the end of the 1920s, the nation's economic roof fell in. The Great Depression of the 1930s, signaled by (but not started by) the stock market crash of October, 1929, led to a need for increased government spending, to provide for various kinds of work relief. By the time that Franklin D. Roosevelt was inaugurated as President of the United States in March of 1933, about the only option for FDR was truly massive Federal spending, financed by a huge Federal deficit. FDR tried to cut the costs of routine government operation to the bone, but his big anti-depression projects were characterized by big deficits.

The end of the Great Depression did not bring about an end to large federal deficits. Instead, the Depression was followed by one crisis after another. First, there was World War II, then the beginning of the Cold War, the Korean Conflict, Viet-Nam, and recently, the War on Terror, one aspect of which was the Iraq War. Along the way, there have been a few "balanced budgets," but not many.

Also along the way, Congress persons have voted repeatedly to raise their salaries, which probably were too low, in relation to other salaries, in the years before World War II especially, but now have gotten to be way too high. Incumbency has gotten to be a way of life for many, as they use a variety of strategies to try to hold onto power and keep their noses stuck in the public feeding trough.

Many Congress persons now routinely use deficit spending to finance public projects for the benefit of their states or districts, then use the fact that they were able to influence such spending as a justification for voters to return them to office so that they can "bring home the bacon" in the form of more projects financed by more deficit spending. This vicious practice just rolls on and on, without restraint. The process causes constant inflation and is increasingly dangerous to the existence of our government.

More than 25 years ago, Congress was being deluged with resolutions from the State legislatures, requesting that a constitutional convention be called for the purpose of drafting a "balance the budget" constitutional amendment. To placate the proponents of a constitutional convention, Congress itself considered several proposed "balance the budget" amendments, and in a handful of instances, came as close as one vote to approving, in either the House or the Senate, an amendment that would allow Congress to engage in deficit spending only with a "super-majority" vote.

I wrote a book, published in 1986, providing guidance to those who were trying to get a constitutional convention. In that book, titled *Great Restraint*, I proposed a "balance the budget" constitutional amendment that would really work to put a stop to deficit spending by the federal government.

Few people read my book. During the course of writing it, I became aware of the fact that Congress itself did not want *any* "balance the budget" amendment, and certainly not one that would actually *work* to bring a halt to deficit spending by the federal government. After it was published, I furnished copies of my book to many members of Congress.

They politely ignored it. And gradually, I realized why.

So, how do we, the people, take away the congressional credit card?

We have to have a constitutional amendment. We can call it a "balance the budget" amendment but what we really need to do is limit the power of Congress to borrow money in normal times, while providing Congress with the power to raise enough money in taxes so that Congress will be able to balance the budget in normal times. We also need to give Congress the power to borrow money in two situations: war; and during a period of great national emergency.

The "balance the budget" amendment draft set forth above is substantially the same as the one proposed in my book, *Great Restraint.* I eliminated a couple of Sections from my original proposal and added a few words here and there in order to clarify some provisions and obviate needless litigation; for example, the exemption from tax for "goods fairly within the ambit of the First Article of Amendment" that I included in Section 8 probably was not needed, but I put it in by way of clarification.

The foregoing proposed amendment should operate to effectively take away the congressional credit card. It is quite possible that in order to get this amendment officially "proposed" within the meaning of the U. S. Constitution, it may be necessary for us--that is, we, the people--to demand a constitutional convention. This was my underlying assumption in writing *Great Restraint*. It was my belief then, and continues to be my belief now, more than two decades later, that Congress probably would not be willing to give up its "credit card" without a struggle, and that it was going to take a constitutional convention to get the job done.

What I found after writing the book was that Congress was not going to propose an effective "balance the budget" amendment" on its own. After my book came out, Congress did make a few more feeble attempts to propose a "balance the budget" amendment" on its own, but none of the attempts were successful, and as I had predicted, the amendments that Congress considered, on its own, would not have been effective, and would not have accomplished the desired result.

Therefore, it was apparently going to take a constitutional convention. However, I also found that Congress was unwilling to cooperate in calling a constitutional convention. Therefore, I drafted the Number Eleven Amendment proposal, *Amending, to Amend,* which is included in this book.

There *should* be no problem in getting Congress to propose my Number Eleven Amendment proposal, and once that amendment, clarifying Article V of the original Constitution, is officially proposed by Congress and ratified by the State legislatures, *as it should be*, so that the congressional monopoly over the amendment process is ended and the rights of the people to have a role in the amendment process are restored, as the Founding Fathers originally intended, then it should be possible to have a constitutional convention for the purpose of officially proposing an effective "balance the budget" amendment" as herein set forth (as my Number Three Amendment proposal).

I know that all of this sounds like it is a little complicated. I agree; but it is not so complicated that we just can't do it. I always come back to this point: The Framers of our wonderful Constitution gave us a plan of government that has served us, very well, for over 200 years. It can keep on serving us well. But, the Framers knew that the Constitution was going to need amending from time to time, and so they provided us with the means to amend it.

As I explained in *Amending, to Amend*, the Framers *intended* for us to use the convention method to amend the constitution, and they just provided that Congress could originate amendments as an afterthought; the Framers had no idea that Congress would monopolize the amendment process as it has done. So just keep this in mind: no matter what anyone may tell you to the contrary, the use of the ***convention*** method to propose amendments was what the Framers intended, and it was the method *they themselves* used to get the Constitution written and adopted in the first place.

If it takes a constitutional convention in order to take away the congressional credit card, then so be it! This may very well be the *only* practical way "To Take Away the Congressional Credit Card!"

The national retail sales tax set forth in Sections 7 and 8 of my proposed amendment is intended as a budget balancing tool, to be used by Congress only to the extent necessary. The national retail sales tax I propose is probably unconstitutional at the present time, but by including it in this proposed constitutional amendment, it would be duly authorized. Proponents of the so-called "Fair Tax" that you may have heard or read about have been pushing for a national retail sales tax that would substitute for the Federal Income Tax. They have been trying to sell a bill of goods to the people of the United States, claiming that their Fair Tax would eliminate the need for the I. R. S. (Internal Revenue Service) and failing to disclose to the people that the U. S. Constitution would have to be amended before the Fair Tax could even be seriously considered.

Rich people, of course, would be the obvious beneficiaries of the Fair Tax, which they would proceed to evade by buying their needs overseas. They would then get even richer.

Quite frankly, the Federal income tax is really the only feasible way of financing the Federal government at the present time. But it is becoming more and more obvious that we can't keep borrowing a trillion dollars a year to keep our government going, and so we are going to have to use a consumption-based tax of some kind in order to balance the budget and stop borrowing.

My version is limited to fifty per cent of Federal spending, which means that it is useful as a budget-balancer, but it is not intended as a replacement for the Federal income tax. Section 8 of my proposal is intended to eliminate the regressive features common to retail sales taxes, and while the retail sales tax I propose would apply to automobiles, it would be possible for Congress to exempt, say, the first $10,000 on the purchase of a car.

I did not like the retail sales tax idea, but I included it because it is the least objectionable way of raising the necessary revenue for the U. S. government to operate without the chronic borrowing that simply has to be stopped if our Federal government is going to survive.

The Federal Income tax is here to stay; anyone suggesting that a sales tax of any kind can be substituted for the income tax is engaging in wishful thinking, or worse. But it is obvious that the highest marginal income tax rate feasible is about 40 per cent. Many of the States tax incomes at a rate of up to about ten per cent, and their interests have to be accommodated.

There are obvious limits on a national retail sales tax. Again, the interests of the States that depend on sales taxes, which are relatively easy to collect, need to be considered. The sales tax I am proposing, as a means of balancing the Federal budget, is probably going to top out at ten per cent or less, and it's obviously a flat rate tax, limited by the exemptions I included in Section 8. Congress is going to have to trim Federal spending. Choices will have to be made.

It will help to take Social Security, and Medicare, out of the Federal budget, as proposed in my amendments Number Four and Five. Social Security has long been financed by a special contribution tax on payrolls. Medicare is a different situation, and continuing it as it has been so far may require some adjustments, one of which may be an increase in the small special tax that has been used in the past to support it.

NUMBER FOUR:

MAKING SOCIAL SECURITY PERMANENT

There is hereby declared to be a permanent, vested retirement system known as the Social Security System. The system is intended to produce a life annuity, paid monthly to eligible citizens of the United States of America, and to others as may be provided by Congress, wherever they are living, commencing upon the age of 70, from a Social Security Trust Fund to which they have contributed for a minimum of 20 years, unless they have been fully and permanently disabled short of 20 years. The Social Security Trust Fund shall not be considered part of the general funds of the government of the United States of America, but payments from the Trust Fund shall be guaranteed by the full faith and credit of the United States. It is the intent of this Amendment that the existing Social Security provisions shall be merged with the provisions hereof.

Contribution tax rates for participants, and their employers, shall be as set by Congress. If funding falls short, Congress shall supplement the fund from general tax revenues. Participants who have contributed 20 or more years may commence annuity payments as early as age 62, with their monthly benefits reduced by four per cent per year for each year of such early payments. Upon death, each participant's estate will be paid a final payment equal to fifty per cent of one month's regular benefit.

All earned income shall be subject to the contribution tax, at uniform tax rates, for the support of the Social Security System. The monthly benefit, per person, shall not exceed either the median or the average monthly benefit that would have been paid to the highest fifty per cent of beneficiaries, plus twelve per cent, if not for this restriction. The contribution tax rates, and the monthly benefits for each person, shall be as set by Congress, based upon the contribution taxes previously paid, and subject to the benefit limitation set forth above.

Benefit payments that would otherwise be payable to incarcerated or involuntarily institutionalized individuals shall be paid to the prison or institution confining such individuals, for their support, except for five per cent which shall be paid to the individual as a personal allowance.

Monthly benefit payments shall not be subject to any individual income tax (Federal, State, or Local), shall not be affected by any other income or assets of the individual beneficiary, and shall not be subject to the claims of creditors.

Congress shall establish a monthly benefit program of payments from the Social Security Trust Fund to or for the benefit of disabled individuals otherwise unable to earn an income for the support of themselves or their lawful dependents. Such monthly benefits shall not exceed the maximum benefit payments to life annuity beneficiaries as set forth above.

Making Social Security a Vested, Constitutional Right

When President Franklin D. Roosevelt signed the bill that established Social Security, in 1935, he assumed that he was setting up a permanent, Federal program that Congress would not dare to eliminate. It was to be financed, mainly, by a "contribution" tax to be paid one-half by the employer, and the other one-half by a deduction from the employee's paycheck.

At the time, FDR explained the financing of Social Security this way: "We put those payroll contributions there so as to give the contributors a legal, moral, and political right to collect their pensions . . . With those taxes in there, no damn politician can ever scrap my social security program."

Not that politicians haven't tried. In the guise of "improving" Social Security, there have been proposals to "privatize" it. And there have been other proposals.

Also, there have been claims that Social Security is underfunded, and will eventually run out of money from which to pay benefits. From the first, there has been a "cap" on the amount of an individual's earnings that are subject to the Social Security tax. The "cap" has been raised from time to time, and there have been proposals to remove the "cap" altogether.

Congress has borrowed heavily from the Social Security Trust Fund, and now finds it increasingly inconvenient to have to pay back the "loans." Also, Congress in recent years has been subjecting Social Security benefits to the Federal income tax, despite the fact that the workers have already paid income tax on their earnings, so are being subject to the income tax on their earnings a second time.

Now that the 2012 election is over with, it is obvious that at least some members of Congress are proposing to reduce "entitlements," including the Social Security benefits that present and future workers are now collecting.

I believe it is time to put the Social Security program out of the reach of Congress and make it a Constitutional Right of the workers for whom Social Security was originally set up. To that end, I drafted the proposed constitutional amendment reproduced above. The language is pretty self-explanatory, but I will now comment on some of the features of my proposal.

The most important feature is to make Social Security a vested, constitutional right. At the present time, Social Security is just a set of laws that Congress can change, or even abolish, at any time. The fact that you may have paid into Social Security for many years does not give you a vested constitutional right to your Social Security benefits. As far as the law is concerned, you have just been paying a tax so that other people can draw Social Security benefits.

By amending the Constitution and establishing your right to your Social Security benefits as a vested, constitutional right, you have something that Congress cannot legally take away. The proposed amendment authorizes Congress to change details such as tax rates and benefit levels, but Congress will no longer be able to raid the Social Security Trust Fund, nor will Congress any longer be able to borrow from the Social Security Trust Fund. My amendment also bars any layer of government from taxing your Social Security benefits. Creditors are also barred from being able to reach your Social Security benefits.

The basic features of Social Security are preserved. Once you have reached the age of 70 and have paid into the Social Security system for 20 years, your benefits are yours for as long as you live. In other words, you have a lifetime annuity, with benefits paid to you wherever you live. You can get reduced benefits as early as age 62, assuming you have contributed for 20 years or more.

The earnings "cap" is eliminated. **All** "earned income" is subject to the Social Security contribution tax. There is an upper level of benefits. In other words, you may have earned millions of dollars, but your Social Security benefits are limited by a formula set forth in the draft proposal.

But your benefits are not "means tested." You get your Social Security benefits, even if you have a lot of other income. This is fair; if you paid into the system for 20 years or more, you get your benefits. Period. If you are in a prison or other institution, involuntarily, your benefits are paid to the institution for your support, except for five per cent which is paid to you as a personal allowance.

The proposal provides benfits for participants who are disabled, even if they are not fully vested yet.

It's now up to the millions of Social Security beneficiaries to use their political power to pursuade members of Congress, and of the State legislatures, to get this amendment adopted.

NUMBER FIVE:

MAKING MEDICARE PERMANENT

There is hereby declared to be a permanent, vested system whereby beneficiaries receive reimbursement, either directly or indirectly, for medical care services provided to them by participating healthcare providers within the United States, known as the Medicare System.

Any U. S. citizen, age 55 or over, who has made contributions to the Medicare system for five years or more, shall be considered an eligible beneficiary. The system shall be supported by a payroll tax on all earned income, paid at uniform equal rates on all employers and employees alike, and by a monthly premium payable by or on behalf of all beneficiaries, which shall be deducted and paid from Social Security payments otherwise payable to Social Security beneficiaries who elect to participate and receive Medicare benefits, which shall not be mandatory and shall not be means-tested.

No healthcare provider shall be required to participate in the Medicare system. Nothing contained herein shall prevent the United States government from participating in the Medicare system by organizing a system or institution(s) for providing healthcare services in competition with other healthcare providers, and for seeking reimbursements from Medicare in the same manner as other, non-governmental healthcare service providers.

All Medicare payments shall be paid into or out of a Medicare Trust Fund that shall not be considered part of the general funds of the government of the United States of America and shall be backed by the full faith and credit of the United States. Tax, benefit, and other details having to do with the Medicare system shall be as provided for by the Congress. There is no need for appropriations to be set by the Congress, since Medicare shall operate on a continuous basis from and after the ratification of this Amendment, and since the existing Medicare system shall be merged with the provisions hereof. At no time shall Medicare limit

payments or reimbursement based upon some particular level on a per-person basis.

It is intended that the level of benefits provided to all individual participants and providers will be essentially uniform throughout the United States, except where some particular condition may indicate to the contrary. The monthly premiums charged to Medicare beneficiaries may be varied by age level but in no event may the premium level exceed ten per cent of the Social Security income of the particular beneficiary. Beneficiaries who are not yet receiving Social Security income shall not be charged a monthly premium.

Making Medicare a Vested, Constitutional Right

In a way, President Franklin D. Roosevelt was the father of Medicare as well as Social Security, even though Medicare was not passed by Congress until Lyndon B. Johnson was president, years after FDR's death. But FDR, as he worked on the Social Security legislation during his first term as president, considered the inclusion of medical care for the elderly as a part of Social Security. He gave up on the idea because he expected massive opposition from the politically powerful AMA (American Medical Association).

President Lyndon Johnson had been a young congressman from Texas, and a former school teacher, when FDR was the newly elected president. Johnson was a U. S. Senator in 1960 when a young fellow senator, John F. Kennedy, won the Democratic presidential nomination and needed a running mate who would help him secure the large block of Texas electoral votes.

Johnson became president when Kennedy was felled by an assassin's bullets in November of 1963.

It could certainly be said that Lyndon Johnson was a disciple of FDR. As president, Lyndon Johnson acknowledged FDR's influence in getting Medicare through Congress. And as it turned out, Medicare had an immediate impact on the Social Security beneficiaries who could now afford to go to the doctor. U. S. average life expectancy took an immediate leap.

Medicare, from the outset, was divided into two parts. Part A was hospital coverage, paid from general tax revenues. Part B was optional medical insurance, which beneficiaries paid for with a monthly premium, deducted from their Social Security benefits.

Medicare proved to be an immediately popular program that was also an expensive entitlement burden for U. S. taxpayers. As a conservative congressman, Paul Ryan had proposed changing the financing of Medicare, prior to becoming Mitt Romney's vice-presidential running mate in 2012. Under Ryan's proposal, Medicare would become a voucher that would help Senior Citizens buy private medical insurance.

This would save taxpayers money but would strip many Medicare beneficiaries from coverage that they had been paying for, by means of the payroll taxes they had contributed, because many would have been unable to pay the premiums for private medical insurance that would only be paid for, in part, by the vouchers. (At the very time this book was published, Congressman Ryan was at it again, proposing Medicare cuts in order to balance the budget, supposedly in ten years. His proposals were nonstarters, as far as Democrats were concerned.)

Democrats wasted no time in massively opposing the Romney/Ryan ticket and the threat the Republican candidates posed to Medicare beneficiaries. In my judgment, this threat was at least partially the cause of the Republicans losing the 2012 election. And after the election, with the Republicans in control of the House of Representatives, efforts to decrease Federal spending on "entitlements," which clearly included Medicare, and threats to eliminate Medicare altogether, were very real.

The recent addition of Medicare Part D, a prescription drug benefit, had run up the bill for Medicare even further than Lyndon Johnson had anticipated. However, substantial cost savings in the operation of the Medicare program were possible, and the Obama administration claimed, at the time of the 2012 election, that such savings were ongoing.

There is no doubt in my mind that President Barack Obama won re-election in 2012, at least partially, with his promises to maintain the Medicare program.

Medicare is not a mirror image of Social Security. Nevertheless, it is clear that Medicare also needs the protection that only a constitutional amendment can give it. It is in that spirit that I propose making Medicare permanent by making it a constitutional right.

NUMBER SIX:

ESTABLISHING THE NATIONAL COURT OF APPEALS

Section 1. There is hereby established a National Court of Appeals, the purpose of which is to decide, on the merits, in summary fashion, based upon Supreme Court precedents, all civil cases filed with the Supreme Court that are not decided on their merits by the Supreme Court. A panel of not fewer than five judges shall decide each case. Appended to the decision in each case shall be a list of Supreme Court decisions that were considered by the panel. Congress shall have the power, at any time, of enlarging the jurisdiction of the National Court of Appeals to include criminal cases filed with the Supreme Court.

Section 2. Decisions by the National Court of Appeals shall not be published nor constitute precedent in this or any other court;

provided, however, they shall be available to the general public and may be published by any interested person or organization. Decisions of the National Court of Appeals shall be given the same effect as decisions of the Supreme Court except insofar as their lack of precedental value, and may be further reviewed by the Supreme Court under rules established thereby.

Section 3. The President, with the advice of the Senate, shall appoint judges to serve on the National Court of Appeals, and on all other Federal Courts including the Supreme Court, for an initial period of ten years only, but such appointments may be renewed by the Senate, acting alone, for as many as four additional terms of ten years each.

Section 4. All Federal judges shall be objectively fair and impartial at all times, and consistent partiality shall constitute grounds for impeachment and removal. A refusal to recuse for such partiality may be appealed immediately. All proceedings in open court shall be video recorded, and such recordings shall be available to parties and the public at nominal cost. On appeal, any litigant may

proceed on the basis of the recording or pertainent part thereof in lieu of the formal record.

Section 5. Juries in trials of capital offenses shall be required to decide upon a unanimous verdict of guilt beyond any doubt whatsoever. The limitations period for all cases in Federal courts shall be five years, or eight years if some provision of this Constitution is involved, unless some other period is specified by the Constitution or by Congress, with tolling permitted, and no State limitations period to be borrowed. There is no limitations period for cases involving the death of a human being, from and after the live birth thereof. *Res judicata* requires an actual prior trial followed by a decision on the merits.

Section 6. No filing fees shall be charged by the National Court of Appeals, and no fees shall be transferred to said court, for its support, by any other court. Appropriations for the support of the National Court of Appeals shall be made by the Congress not less often than annually, and in default of such appropriations, the Clerk of the National

Court of Appeals, who shall be appointed by the President with the advice of the Senate to serve for a five year term, renewable by the Senate for additional five year terms, shall draw from the Treasury sufficient funds to keep the court operating until Congress itself makes appropriations therefor.

Section 7. The National Court of Appeals shall not hear oral arguments and shall be housed in existing U.S. Courthouse space within the District of Columbia until such time as Congress provides specific space for the court.

Section 8. This amendment shall be fully effective for all pending cases upon the date of its ratification.

Why We Need a National Court of Appeals: The Disgraceful "Constitutional Rights" Scam

In recent years, an average of about 8,000 cases per year have been filed with the United States Supreme Court. Of these, about 6,000 cases, or about 75 per cent, have been filed "in forma pauperis", without payment of the "normal" $300 docket fee; most of these are prisoner cases.

Also in recent years, the United States Supreme Court has actually heard, and decided, fewer than 100 cases per year. Here I will quote from the 2006 Year-End Report on the Federal Judiciary by Chief Justice John Roberts:

> During the 2005 Term, 87 cases were argued and 82 were disposed of in 69 signed opinions, compared to 87 cases argued and 85 disposed of in 74 signed opinions in the 2004 Term.

> No cases from the 2005 Term were scheduled for reargument in the 2006 Term.

So according to the Chief Justice, only about 85 cases were actually decided per year, but for purposes of this discussion, I'll be generous and continue to use the figure of 100 cases per year.

In his Year-End Report, the Chief Justice did not express any shock or dismay about the 7,900 or so cases that the Supreme Court did *not* decide; on the contrary, except for some statistics, the Chief Justice devoted his entire report to a plea, mainly addressed to Congress, to raise federal judicial pay.

Since he didn't, I will--talk about the 7,900 or so cases per year that the U. S. Supreme Court is *not* deciding.

This is a problem that has developed over time. Over a period of more than 200 years, since the U. S. Constitution was first put into operation in 1789, with George Washington as president, who then appointed John Jay as Chief Justice of the United States, with five other judges appointed as associate justices.

The first U. S. Census, in 1790, showed a total population for the new nation as 3,929,214, or in round figures, just under four million. The U. S. Census, in the year 2000, showed a total U. S. population of 291,421,906, again in round figures, just under 292 million. (The U. S. population now exceeds 313 million.)

The nation began with six justices on the Supreme Court; now we have nine. And we have had nine for more than a century. So we have increased our nation's size, in population, by about 300 million, while increasing the size of our nation's highest court by three justices.

To put it another way: we began the United States, under the Constitution of 1787, with just eleven States (Rhode Island and North Carolina had not ratified the Constitution by the time the new government got underway, so it started without them). The United States now consists of 50 States, plus the District of Columbia.

Another measure: we began the United States with just the Constitution as originally written in 1787, and ratified by eleven States, but without the Bill of Rights comprising the first ten amendments to the U. S. Constitution. The first U. S. Congress proposed twelve amendments to the Constitution on September 25, 1789, and sent them out to the States for ratification. Ten of them were declared to have been ratified as of December 15, 1791, and they became known as the Bill of Rights.

Of the other two amendments proposed by Congress in 1789, one quickly became obsolete because of increases in population, and the other one was ratified more than 200 years later, becoming the 27th and most recent amendment to the Constitution, but obviously not a part of the Bill of Rights. (For the story of the 27th Amendment, see the Notes for the Epilogue, in the very back of this book.)

As the judicial power of the "new" United States of America began to be exercised, some problems arose with the way that the original Constitution (without the Bill of Rights, of course) had been drafted, so Congress, almost immediately, had to propose another amendment, the Eleventh Amendment, to remedy the situation. The Eleventh Amendment was proposed March 4, 1794 and was declared ratified February 7, 1795, eleven months later, very quick action considering the speed of transportation and communication at that time. It had taken more than two years to get the Bill of Rights ratified.

The first presidential election involving someone other than George Washington and John Adams revealed another mistake that the Framers had made, in drafting the Constitution, necessitating another amendment, the Twelfth Amendment, proposed by Congress on December 9, 1803, and declared ratified the following summer, July 27, 1804, less than eight months later.

The Constitution was not amended again until after the Civil War, although there were many attempts to amend it, before that time, in order to try to do away with slavery.

In the years following the Civil War, when it became obvious that the Supreme Court was unable to keep up with the growth in litigation as the nation expanded, Congress established the circuit appellate courts, to handle appeals from the federal District Courts so that the Supreme Court could deal with the most important cases. Today, there are thirteen circuits, twelve of which are regional, and each of which has a U. S.

Court of Appeals, some of which meet in more than one location.

In the 8th Circuit where I live, for example, the U. S. Court of Appeals for the 8th Circuit holds court in St. Louis, Missouri, and in St. Paul, Minnesota.

The judges of the regional appellate courts are ordinarily drawn from the District Courts of the region; they are appointed by the President, of course (as are Supreme Court Justices) and confirmed by the U. S. Senate.

In theory, all federal judges take an oath to support the Constitution of the United States. And the Supreme Court is supposed to be the final arbiter of what the Constitution means. An immense body of Supreme Court precedent exists. It would seem obvious that the lower Federal courts would follow the precedents set by the Supreme Court.

They do. Sometimes. Sometimes not.

In each of the circuits, the Court of Appeals for that circuit also establishes precedent. Sometimes these precedents conflict with precedents set in other circuits. When that happens, the Supreme Court can sometimes be persuaded to consider a case in order to resolve a conflict among the circuits.

Also, sometimes a decision by one of the Court of Appeals appears to conflict with a decision by the Supreme Court. In such a case, the Supreme Court will sometimes bring the case up for review.

But notice I used the word "sometimes." The Supreme Court simply does not have time to deal with all of the conflicts among the circuits, or with the decisions of lower courts, that appear to conflict with decisions of the Supreme Court. Or, for that matter, with provisions of the Constitution, or of federal statutes. And then, there are the decisions of the state appellate courts.

In theory, the U. S. Supreme Court is over all of the highest courts of each of the fifty States. In practice, even in cases where the U. S. Constitution is invoked, the Supreme Court of the United States rarely takes notice. It lacks the time to do so.

Early In 1937, President Franklin D. Roosevelt, noting the increased workload of the United States Supreme Court, proposed enlarging the Court by appointing several additional associate justices. Some of FDR's political opponents accused him of trying to "pack" the Court in order to keep it from invalidating his "New Deal" legislation (which, of course, is exactly why he was proposing to enlarge the Court), and when his proposal to enlarge the Court went to Congress, FDR suffered the greatest defeat of his political career. As far as I know, no president since then has even breathed the possibility of enlarging the Supreme Court.

To deal with the Court's business today would take something like 450 Supreme Court Justices. Sitting in panels of six, the size of the Court originally, the Supreme Court might be able to handle the problems of a nation of 300 million-plus, but it wouldn't be the same. We would have 75 Supreme Courts instead of just one, an obviously unworkable situation.

Each of the regional Courts of Appeal produces decisions which constitute precedent within their own regions. But only the Supreme Court can produce the authoritative, nationwide precedents which the nation as a whole requires. Imagine the chaos that would result if we had twelve regional appellate courts producing *conflicting* decisions on a subject such as abortion! Actually, we do have such chaos, ***right now!***

The Framers of our Constitution couldn't have imagined our present situation, where the Supreme Court picks fewer than100 cases a year to hear and decide, and denies any review at all to the 7,900 other cases on its docket. In other words, the Founding Fathers never contemplated a Supreme Court to which no ordinary citizen would have access.

I'm going to describe to you now an actual U. S. Supreme Court case that I handled some time back, in order to demonstrate what I am here calling the "Constitutional Rights" scam. The word "scam" is defined by the dictionary as "a fraudulent or deceptive act or operation." (By the way, the scam here is the fault of Congress, not the Supreme Court, as I will explain, later.)

Here is the Seventh Amendment to the United States Constitution, part of the Bill of Rights, one of the constitutional rights supposedly guaranteed to every American citizen:

> In suits at common law, where the value in controversy shall exceed twenty dollars, the right of trial by jury shall be preserved, and no fact tried by a jury shall be otherwise reexamined in any court of the United States, than according to the rules of the common law.

The plaintiff, in a U. S. District Court case, made it plain, early on, that she wanted her civil suit for damages tried before a jury. She was thus asserting her constitutional right, *guaranteed her by the Seventh Amendment, U. S. Constitution,* to a trial by jury! It is important to realize that no court had any right whatsoever to substitute some other kind of a trial or other procedure for her jury trial right. And yet, that is *exactly* what the U. S. District Court did to her, and got away with it! How could that happen?

It was a long, somewhat complicated case, that played out over a five year period. To keep this short, I'll simply tell you that the plaintiff objected, over and over, to being denied her jury trial. The U. S. District Court judge simply said, "She is not entitled to a jury trial . . ." When summary judgment was entered against her, she then filed an appeal with the U. S. Court of Appeals for the 8th Circuit. Amazingly, that Court ruled against her, affirming the District Court, and totally ignoring her jury trial rights! She sought rehearing, and again, the Court of Appeals ignored her jury trial rights, so there was no possibility that this was simply a mistake by the Court of Appeals. Obviously, the Court of Appeals *meant to deny her constitutional right to a jury trial!*

This couldn't happen in America--right? *It could not happen!* But it did. And now I'll tell you "the rest of the story."

The plaintiff then filed what is known as a "petition for a writ of certiorari" with the United States Supreme Court. This is the procedure most used, nowadays, to attempt to obtain Supreme Court review of a lower court decision, regardless of whether it is a federal court decision or a state court decision. In her petition for certiorari, on the jury trial point, plaintiff said, in pertinent part:

> The Court of Appeals totally ignored petitioner's Seventh Amendment

> Constitutional right to a jury trial in sustaining the District Court's summary judgment . . .

Here is the point upon which the Supreme Court should have ruled, reversing the Court of Appeals and sending the case back to the District Court for a jury trial--by another Judge--citing the Seventh Amendment, U. S. Constitution. The District Court, and the 8th Circuit, clearly had violated plaintiff's constitutional right to a jury trial. But the certiorari procedure is not really the same as an appeal, which is now available, to the U. S. Supreme Court, in only very limited circumstances.

As Supreme Court Rule 10 now states,

> Review on a writ of certiorari is not a matter of right, but of judicial discretion. A petition for a writ of certiorari will be granted only for compelling reasons. . . .

You may be surprised to learn that total denial of a Seventh Amendment Constitutional right, or indeed of any of the other rights *guaranteed* by the U. S. Constitution, is *not* one of the "compelling reasons" spelled out in Supreme Court Rule 10.

It takes the affirmative vote of four of the nine U. S. Supreme Court Justices to get a writ of certiorari from the U. S. Supreme Court.

Each case is presented to the members of the Court in a closed-door conference. Such presentations each last but a few seconds and then a quick vote is taken; only about *one* case out of every *one hundred* cases gets the required four votes. Supreme Court Rule 16, paragraph 3 states that

> Whenever the Court denies a petition for a writ of certiorari, [and this is what happens to about 99 cases out of every 100] the Clerk will prepare, sign, and enter an order to that effect and will notify forthwith counsel of record and the court whose judgment was sought to be reviewed. . . .

As a practical matter, the order entered by the Clerk, disposing of the case, simply gives the number and title of the case and then the two words "certiorari denied." That's all it says. But what it means is that the lower court's decision remains unchanged by the U. S. Supreme Court, so in the case I've been describing, it meant, to the plaintiff, that the Supreme Court wasn't going to correct the lower court's denial of her jury trial right, even though her jury trial right was supposedly guaranteed her by the U. S. Constitution, and even though all the U. S. Supreme Court had to do was order the lower court to give her a jury trial. Which it could have done with no more effort than what she actually got: "certiorari denied." All because the U. S. Supreme Court "did not have time" to consider her case "on the merits," as lawyers say.

There was a time, before William H. Rehnquist became Chief Justice, when the U. S. Supreme Court would occasionally use its inherent power to summarily dispose of a case on the merits, a power the Court still has; see Rule 16, paragraph 1. The late Chief Justice Rehnquist, however, rather famously said, on a number of occasions, that he was opposed to having the Supreme Court deal with any but the most important cases; in his view, the Court's time was too valuable to "waste" any of it on what he considered to be trivial cases. So far as I am aware, Chief Justice Roberts has not departed from the rather exalted position taken by Chief Justice Rehnquist. In fact, when reading his previously cited Annual Report, I was particularly struck by the elitist position he expressed with regard to judicial salaries:

> Our judiciary will not properly serve its constitutional role if it is restricted to (1) persons so wealthy that they can afford to be indifferent to the level of judicial compensation, or (2) people for whom the judicial salary represents a pay increase.

Chief Justice Roberts continued:

> Do not get me wrong--there are very good judges in both of those categories. But a judiciary drawn more and more from only those categories would not be the sort of judiciary on which we have historically depended to protect the rule of law in this country.

It should be obvious, from the foregoing discussion, that the U. S. Supreme Court is not going to concern itself with any of the 7,900 cases that it does not have time to handle each year. And Congress is not going to appoint the 450 or so additional Justices that it would take to handle the case load. In case you missed the point that I was earlier leading up to, 450 Justices, sitting in panels of six would be 75 panels; if each one handled about 100 cases a year, we would have 75 x 100= 7,500 cases, which is very close to the 7,900 cases a year that the Supreme Court, as presently constituted, does not have time to handle.

I want to make it clear beyond any doubt, however, that I am *not* suggesting the appointment of 450 additional Supreme Court Justices. Also, I want to make it clear that I am *not* suggesting that the Supreme Court itself decide those 7,900 cases a year by means of summary dispositions. I would note that even in the past, before Chief Justice Rehnquist, the Supreme Court disposed of only a few additional cases by means of summary dispositions.

However, something *does* need to be done. Because, at present, the ordinary person has no way of enforcing his or her constitutional rights. And since those rights cannot be enforced, as a practical matter, those rights simply do not exist.

That's why the original title of this article was *The "Constitutional Rights" Scam*. That's what constitutional rights are, at the present time, for the ordinary person; they are a fraud, a scam. They are on paper but they are not real, because there is no mechanism for enforcing them. The Courts, the Judges, are supposed to enforce them. But they don't. Oh, sometimes they do. And as plaintiff's case demonstrates, sometimes they don't. You can't depend on the Courts to enforce them. They can be denied by judicial whim, or by the Court's simply ignoring them, as we saw the 8th Circuit Court of Appeals do, in plaintiff's case.

And when we get to the Supreme Court, we find that the Supreme Court does not have time to handle the ordinary person's case. Remember Rule 10, quoted earlier; the Supreme Court won't even consider your case unless you have "compelling reasons," and mere denial of a constitutional right does *not* constitute a "compelling reason."

Who is at fault? How have our constitutional rights been lost? Who can do anything about this situation?

The answer is set forth in the U. S. Constitution, Article III, Section 1, which gives Congress the power and the duty to establish "inferior courts" (which are all of the federal courts below the level of the U. S. Supreme Court). Congress established the U. S. District Courts.

Congress established the circuit appellate courts. All of the judges of these courts take an oath to support the Constitution. But often, they don't. At the merest whim, they can, and do, ignore constitutional rights. That's why thousands of cases are filed with the United States Supreme Court every year. And as we have seen, the Supreme Court can handle fewer than 100 cases a year.

The solution? A new appellate court, one that can and will handle, in summary fashion, all of the cases that are filed with the Supreme Court but which the Supreme Court doesn't have time to handle. Most of these cases involve the alleged denial of constitutional (or statutory) rights. Most of these cases need a decision, such as a decision that, yes, constitutional rights have been violated, and something should be done about it; in plaintiff's case, for example, the decision should have been that, yes, plaintiff was entitled to a jury trial, and she didn't get one, so the District Court decision denying her a jury trial should be reversed and the case sent back to the District Court for a jury trial. And it probably would be best to direct the District Court to have a different judge handle her jury trial, because the judge who denied her a jury trial for no reason at all, just a whim, will probably treat her unfairly in other ways, if we let him handle her jury trial.

So, I propose that Congress establish a new, National Court of Appeals. It would be given the job of taking *all* of the cases that the U. S. Supreme Court does not have time to handle, and deciding them, on the merits, but in a brief, summary fashion, applying U. S. Supreme Court precedents. For example, when the Supreme Court issues an order denying a writ of certiorari, the case would then be sent over to the National Court of Appeals. Here, a federal judge on the National Court of Appeals would propose rulings with respect to the points set forth in the petition for certiorari, and would propose a summary disposition of the case such as "reversed," "affirmed," etc. If the judge found that briefs needed to be submitted, he or she could call for them to be filed pursuant to existing Supreme

Court Rules (such as Rule 24). When the judge handling the case had it ready for disposition, he or she would bring it to the attention of one of the five-judge panels of the National Court of Appeals which would *not* include the judge who had been preparing the case for disposition. In most instances, the disposition of the case could be handled in no more than one working day, and on the basis of the presentation made in the petition for certiorari. The panel of judges would make the actual disposition of the case, but without a formal written opinion. An order would go out from the National Court of Appeals directly to the court that needed to take further action in the case, normally the U. S. District Court or the State appellate court. That court would be told what action it should take, such as ordering a jury trial, as in the case I was using as an example. The previous judgment by the lower court would be ordered vacated or reversed.

The fundamental duty of the National Court of Appeals would be to see to it that the people of the United States are accorded their rights under the U. S. Constitution and the other laws of the United States. By setting up this means of vindicating such rights, Congress would put an end to the present constitutional rights scam, which exists only because Congress has so far failed to carry out its duties with respect to Article III, Section 1, of the U. S. Constitution.

It is quite possible that many members of Congress are unaware of the constitutional rights scam that I have here described. But now that I have alerted them as to the true situation--a situation they can verify by simply crossing the street to the Supreme Court Building, going to the Clerk's office, and reading some of the petitions for certiorari that have been denied in recent months--I would hope they see the need for the new National Court of Appeals that I have here proposed.

I want to tell you about another case that I had, just a few months ago, that illustrates the need for the National Court of Appeals.

In the wake of the Civil War, Congress proposed the Fourteenth Amendment to the U. S. Constitution. The Fourteenth Amendment included five numbered Sections. Sections 2, 3, and 4 had to do, mostly, with the Southern States that had been in rebellion, so that these sections of the Fourteenth Amendment are little more than historical relics.

Section 1, however, is without doubt one of the most important parts of what we think of when we think of the Constitutional rights that are supposed to be the rights of all of us under the U. S. Constitution. For practical purposes, all of our modern civil rights laws are based upon Section 1 of the Fourteenth Amendment.

To cite just one example: all of the massive litigation having to do with the elimination of public school segregation, beginning with *Brown v. Board of Education* in 1954, was based on Section 1 of the Fourteenth Amendment.

Section 5 of the Fourteenth Amendment provided that "Congress shall have power to enforce, by appropriate legislation, the provisions of this article."

Following the ratification of the Fourteenth Amendment, in 1868, Congress passed a variety of laws, pursuant to Section 5 of the Fourteenth Amendment. Some of those laws are gone now, for one reason or another. But one of those laws that still exists is now codified as 42 U. S. Code,

Section 1983. That means it is set forth in part 42 of the United States Code, and it is Section 1983 of that part.

The wording of Section 1983 is quite specific. It has been involved in literally thousands of civil rights cases. Thousands of judges have interpreted Section 1983, but not all judges have interpreted it the same way. In fact, in one famous case, decided in 1989, the Supreme Court ruled that State officials (obviously "officials" are persons, human beings) were **not** ***persons*** for purposes of Section 1983! Since the defendants in my case **were** persons, I didn't want to rely on Section 1983, because they were persons who were acting in both official and personal capacities. I was relying on Section 1 of the Fourteenth Amendment itself, which did not use the word "person" in either sense.

I was using a modern jurisdictional statute, 28 U. S. Code Section 1331, which said, in so many words, that "The district courts shall have original jurisdiction of all civil actions arising under the Constitution ...of the United States." But in my case, the District Court Judge said I could not bring my case directly under the Constitution (even though Section 1331 clearly said I could) and so he dismissed my case, and the Eighth Circuit upheld the district court Judge.

Now the Eighth Circuit, one of the regional appellate courts created by Congress, and supposedly subordinate to the U. S. Supreme Court, has created its own body of precedent. The Eighth Circuit is comprised of the States of Minnesota, North Dakota, South Dakota, Nebraska, Missouri, Arkansas, and my State, Iowa. Thus, in seven States, with a population of more than twenty million people, Federal law, including the U. S. Constitution, is whatever the Eighth Circuit says it is, unless the Supreme Court says otherwise, which it very rarely does because it simply does not have time to do so.

In essence, what the Eighth Circuit Court of Appeals has done, insofar as relevant here, is to build up its own body of precedent which means that, in these States, a litigant who wishes to bring a case under the Fourteenth Amendment, Section 1, cannot do so; he must, instead, bring it under 42 U. S. Code, Section 1983, which Congress enacted pursuant to Section 5 of the Fourteenth Amendment. If he seeks to bring his case directly under the Fourteenth Amendment, Section 1, as clearly authorized by another

Federal statute, enacted by Congress, 28 U. S. Code Section 1331, his case will be dismissed. At least, it will probably be dismissed if he tries to do this in Eighth Circuit-land.

But wait. Can't he appeal the adverse Eighth Circuit ruling to the U. S. Supreme Court?

That's what the Founding Fathers expected, as we see in Article III of the original U. S. Constitution. But we can't now do as the Founding Fathers intended, because the Supreme Court that they provided for in Article III is swamped. I took my case to the U. S. Supreme Court, and this, in pertinent part, is exactly what I said:

> This Court should resolve the question as to whether 42 U. S. Code Section 1983 is, or is not, a prerequisite for consideration of a claim under the Fourteenth Amendment, U. S. Constitution.

I knew, in advance, what the Court's answer should be. No U. S. Supreme Court case has ever decided that 42 U. S. Code Section 1983 is a prerequisite for consideration of a claim under the Fourteenth Amendment, U. S. Constitution, but according to the Eighth Circuit, Section 1983 **is** such a prerequisite! I cited a number of U. S. Supreme Court cases in support of my contention, including—you guessed it, the famous case of *Brown v. Board of Education.*

And what did I get for my effort, bringing this case to the U. S. Supreme Court, (the client, of course, paying the $300 filing fee)?

Nothing, but a polite little note saying that *certiorari* had been denied. No decision on the merits at all.

The real tragedy here is the fact that the litigant, an ordinary citizen of the United States, got no decision from the U. S. Supreme Court. Her constitutional rights had been denied by the Eighth Circuit, treated as nonexistent. The whole thing was just a scam.

Think of it. As a U. S. citizen, you have ***absolutely no constitutional rights at all, because your constitutional rights are unenforceable!***

The National Court of Appeals, proposed here, will effectively restore your constitutional rights.

Just read the proposed amendment and see how it works; you **will** get a decision, based on **Supreme Court** precedent.

I included some other reforms. All Federal judges, including U. S. Supreme Court judges, will have renewable, ten-year terms. No more unaccountable judges, with lifetime appointments. Good judges will have no trouble being reappointed; poor judges will not merit reappointment. All Federal judges will be required, by law, to be impartial. All proceedings in open court will be videotaped, and the videotaped records can be used on appeal, in lieu of the vastly more expensive formal record. And, very important in capital cases, the jury must find the accused guilty "beyond any doubt whatsoever." That would pretty much do away with situations where an accused is convicted, and executed, by means of trumped up evidence. The conviction of anyone accused of a capital crime on the basis of a sham trial is a blot on our civilization and simply cannot be condoned

Under the terms of my Number Six amendment proposal, the president would make the initial appointment of Federal judges, as is the case at the present time, but the Senate, acting alone, would make the decision to *renew* judicial appointments for additional periods of ten years. Also, the Senate would make the decision *not* to renew the appointments of some judges. I considered the idea of having both houses of Congress involved in the renewal of judicial appointments but decided against it. The Senate has a Judiciary Committee that advises the president on appointments of judges now, and I reasoned that this committee is best equipped to keep tabs on the ongoing performance of Federal judges and to make decisions as to whether particular judges merit reappointment—or not. Also, Senators, with staggered six-year terms, are in a better position to handle judicial reappointments than are members of the House, each of whom is up for election every two years.

I included a provision in Section 5 that establishes a standard five-year statute of limitations for Federal court cases unless the Constitution is involved, in which case it is eight years, unless the Constitution, or Congress, provides otherwise. Federal courts now spend a lot of time considering what statute of limitations to use because most of the time, Congress doesn't provide for one, leaving the courts to decide, and they are all over the place, sometimes "borrowing" a State period of limitations, and *they* are also all over the place!

Besides being confusing, the present system makes Federal courts very unpredictable. There is simply no good reason for such inefficiency to continue, when it is so easy to fix. The five year (or eight year) limitations provisions are somewhat arbitrary, which is why I put in a word about "tolling" being permitted; that way, the judge can permit additional time, depending on the factual situation in a particular case, without making the limitations period so long as to allow a lot of "stale" cases to be litigated. In the general run of cases, five years (or eight years if the Constitution is involved) is enough, but there are always exceptional situations, so some judicial discretion is in order. And there is plenty of Supreme Court precedent on limitations available, which the National Court of Appeals can rely on, as appropriate.

Application of the doctrine known as *res judicata* (the case has previously been decided) requires a prior decision based on a trial that was on the merits. What we can expect from the National Court of Appeals is fair decisions, by impartial judges, based on **Supreme Court precedent,** in all cases. We will all be better off when all of us are accorded the constitutional rights that we are all supposed to have.

NUMBER SEVEN:

ABOLISHING THE DOCTRINE OF SOVEREIGN IMMUNITY

The doctrine of sovereign immunity from suit in Federal Court is hereby abolished. The Eleventh Article of Amendment is hereby repealed. No Federal Court shall be deprived of jurisdiction in any case otherwise properly before it by any assertion of immunity from suit by or on behalf of any of the States of the United States, or by or on behalf of any District comprising the seat of government of the United States, or any territory, commonwealth, or other governmental unit considered to be part of the United States, or any political or other subdivision thereof, or the United States government itself. All abrogations of such immunity by the Congress shall be considered valid in any Federal Court. In any suit involving any part of this Constitution, it shall be sufficient to cite the Constitution itself without citing any

particular statute. This Amendment shall be effective for all cases, including pending cases, immediately upon its ratification.

Is It True That the King Can Do No Wrong?

This is the twenty-first century in the United States of America, right? Of course!

Then, why are we still acting like we are living in England in the seventeenth century? Despite numerous attempts by the Congress of the United States to bring our legal system up to date, the United States Supreme Court ***majority*** is still dragging its collective feet, still treating Us, the people of the United States, as though we are still beholden to some king.

Believe it or not, the Supreme Court still treats as controlling precedent a poorly-reasoned and documented opinion it issued in 1890. In doing so, the Supreme Court acts as though the Fourteenth Amendment of the United States Constitution does not exist.

It is time to bring an end to such foolishness. There is only one way to do it, and that is by amending the U. S. Constitution to make it clear to the Supreme Court that this **is** the twenty-first century and we do not have a king.

The way it is now, if your employer is considered to be a part of any State government, and you are wrongfully fired from your job, you can't effectively sue your employer in a Federal Court.

Let's say your employer is a State university, or a State hospital. Let's say further that your supervisor wants to get rid of you, for any reason. They can fire you, without any hearing. Your attorney can file suit in a Federal Court on your behalf, citing discrimination of some kind such as sex discrimination, age discrimination, racial discrimination, etc.

And then, this is what will happen: the attorney representing your employer will file a motion to dismiss your suit on grounds of sovereign immunity. The Judge probably will grant the motion to dismiss, and you will be out of there!

You can have the best case in the world. Let's say you are a woman, and your supervisor was a man who loved to fondle your brests. Clearly sexual harassment. You file a grievance and you wind up getting fired. You can file a lawsuit, but you may not be able to win it because, remember, *the king can do no wrong!* But, you say, we don't have a king. Correction: you don't think we have a king. However, the legal system thinks we still have a king, even though we have *never* had a king, here in the United States.

The problem is that the Founding Fathers who set up our government essentially imported the whole English legal system, king and all. And that means that all this time, we have been stuck with the English concept that the king can do no wrong.

In the English legal system, the king was the government. The concept that the government—the king—could do no wrong was imbedded in the legal system that we imported.

When the U. S. Constitution was originally written, in the summer of 1787, the men who wrote it included no mention of a king. They knew all about the English king, of course, and they had just finished fighting the Revolutionary War, which was aimed at getting the former English colonies out from under the jurisdiction of the English king.

But what happened was this. In an early lawsuit, one of the parties was one of the State governments. The U. S. Supreme Court ruled against the State government. In a panic, some of the State powers that be got Congress to quickly propose the Eleventh Amendment to the U. S. Constitution, which the State governments of the time quickly approved. Here is what the Eleventh Amendment said:

> The judicial power of the United States shall not be construed to extend to any suit in law or equity, commenced or prosecuted against one of the United States by citizens of another State, or by citizens or subjects of any foreign State.

The Eleventh Amendment was approved by Congress on March 4, 1794, and was declared to have been ratified on February 7, 1795. Notice that the Eleventh Amendment, as written, does not bar suits against a State government by citizens of that very State. When that situation came up before the Supreme Court in 1890, the Court ignored the wording of the Eleventh Amendment.

The Court went back to some of the writings of the Founding Fathers that predated the Constitution and ruled that they really meant to include the whole sovereign immunity concept in the Constitution they had written, they had just unintentionally left it out. So, in the 1890 case, the U. S. Supreme Court essentially ignored the actual wording of the Eleventh Amendment and put the whole sovereign immunity thing into the U. S. Constitution. We've been stuck with it, ever since.

In some cases, as many as four members of the U. S. Supreme Court have tried to get rid of sovereign immunity, but the majority of the Court has kept it in. Congress has, on many occasions, attempted to get rid of at least some of the aspects of sovereign immunity; sometimes the Supreme Court has gone along with Congress on this, and sometimes it hasn't.

What we have, then, is a hodgepodge of legal decisions by the Supreme Court, which the justices have to wade through every time the subject of sovereign immunity comes up, which is quite often.

A Constitutional Amendment such as the one I have proposed would allow the Supreme Court to dispense with sovereign immunity once and for all. The Court could actually handle a lot more cases if it didn't have to keep tangling with the whole notion of whether, or not, the king can do no wrong!

The very last provision was aimed at putting an end to a practice by some of the lower Federal Courts that insist a lawsuit cannot be based on the Constitution itself, thus ignoring the wording of 28 U. S. Code Section 1331, which clearly states the contrary.

NUMBER EIGHT:

NO DEFAULT

All bonds, notes, or other interest-bearing debt obligations of the United States government are hereby declared to be not subject to default and will be paid, according to the terms thereof, without regard to any debt limitation or other failure by the Congress of the United States to pass any appropriation or other legislation providing for the payment of such obligations according to the terms thereof. All of such obligations are to be considered backed by the full faith and credit of the United States government and the United States Treasury shall have a permanent duty to see to it that payments thereof shall be made in a timely manner from funds flowing into the Treasury, ahead of all other obligations, and without need of any legislation or authorization other than this provision.

No Default on U. S. Government Debt Obligations

During the summer of 2011, with the 2012 presidential campaign in full swing, there arose a controversy about extending the debt ceiling, with some candidates expressing a no-compromise position; they would actually see the United States defaulting on its bonds rather than voting, in Congress, to once again accomodate further borrowing by the U. S. government.

Default was put off by temporizing, but U. S. government debt obligations were downgraded by bond ratings firms.

There is no excuse for the U. S. government to be put in this position, merely because posturing politicians want to make a political point. I drafted this amendment proposal to make it clear that no matter what Congress did or did not do, the U. S. government would **not** default on its debt obligations. The U. S. Treasury would be authorized, permanently, to pay its debt obligations out of funds flowing into the Treasury.

This is not subject to controversy, and Congress should pass this proposed amendment and get it out to the States for ratification without delay.

NUMBER NINE:

NO MANDATE TO BUY HEALTH INSURANCE

No resident of the United States shall be compelled, in any way, to buy any type of health or medical insurance. The Congress of the United States does not have the power to levy any type of tax or fee on any type of health or medical insurance policy purchased by any resident of the United States from any private company that sells or offers to sell such insurance. Nor shall the Congress have the power to fine or tax any individual resident for his or her failure or refusal to buy health or medical insurance. No Court in the United States shall have jurisdiction over any suit to enforce any tax or demand that is contrary to this Amendment, which shall be effective immediately upon its ratification.

Eliminating the Obamacare Mandate to Buy Health Insurance

The obnoxious mandate to buy health insurance, coupled with the relatively easy way out to simply pay a tax penalty, means that the mandate will not, in fact, greatly expand the number of Americans who will have health insurance in place when they need it. Thus, even though the mandate technally survived the big legal challenge in the June, 2012 Supreme Court decision, the mandate should be repealed, and another approach should be tried. This is what I was talking about when I advocated *selective repeal* of Obamacare. The advantage of accomplishing *selective repeal* by means of a constitutional amendment is that the president has no role in amending the U. S. Constitution. In other words, President Obama does not have to sign it, and he can't veto it. All Congress does is pass it, by a two-thirds vote in each House, and then it goes to the States for ratification.

In the first edition of the book you are now reading, I suggested an alternate to the Obamacare approach, which I will print here:

It really isn't health insurance that the uninsured need. What they need is access to medical care. Having a health insurance card is just the ticket of admission to the medical care system. In this article, I'm going to describe a plan whereby all U. S. residents can have access to the medical care they need, *without* health insurance. Right now, my plan is just a proposal. It will be up to the people--the voters--to decide whether they like my proposal well enough to require the politicians to make it a reality.

Here's my proposal, in just five words: Enlarge the Public Health Service. And now, I'll elaborate, give you the details, tell you how it can work to make quality medical care available to *all* U. S. residents. The first thing to understand is this: My plan does *not* involve health insurance! It does not affect Medicare or Medicaid, and it does not affect existing health insurance.

The U. S. Public Health Service has been around for a long time, more than two centuries.

Originally, it was a sort of medical service for seamen and was under the Treasury Department. Today, the PHS (as I'll refer to it from now on) is part of the U. S. Department of Health and Human Services. The PHS has about 50,000 Civil Service employees. But the PHS *also* has a uniformed medical service, and it is *this* part of the PHS that I am talking about greatly expanding.

The Commissioned Corps of the PHS enjoys some operational similarities to the military services. At the present time, there are about 6,000 Commissioned Corps officers in the PHS and they provide medical services to some specialized populations, such as Native Americans. My proposal envisions enlarging the Commissioned Corps of the PHS and giving it an expanded mission: to provide medical services to all U. S. residents who do not have health insurance (but people who did have health insurance would also be able to use the PHS if they wished to do so; they wouldn't be disqualified just because they had health insurance).

Here's how my proposal would work: The PHS would open at least 200 new facilities to begin with, and would expand further as needed. From the very beginning, each state would have at least two PHS "offices" and big states like Texas and California would have more. Initially, PHS offices would be located essentially next door to existing hospital emergency rooms. Free standing PHS offices would come later.

Any U. S. resident could walk into a PHS office and receive medical care as needed. The patient would pay ten dollars per visit, but if the patient didn't have the ten dollars, it would not be a problem. Every patient would be given a card and an envelope. The patient's name and ID number would go on the card; the card and the ten dollars would go into the envelope and be dropped in a slot. If the patient didn't have the ten dollars, the patient would just note that on the card. The medical personnel treating the patient would not even know whether the patient paid or not; that would be entirely confidential.

Every PHS patient would have his medical record with him, encoded on a plastic card the size of a credit card. At check-in, the patient would produce his medical record card. (If his card were not available, the PHS computer would be able to produce a new card for the patient in a jiffy.) The card would be updated on every visit to a PHS office.

The PHS offices would have nothing to do with insurance. They would not take insurance payments for PHS services. They would not process insurance claims. The savings from not dealing with insurance would be enormous. The PHS offices would not do billing and would not take credit cards, either.

The U. S. government would build a PHS Medical Academy that would be similar to the military academies, such as West Point and Annapolis. The PHS Academy would be located on a large campus somewhere in the midwest and it would also be the site of a huge new teaching hospital. Hospital patients would be flown in from all over the U. S. They would receive care in the hospital at the rate of ten dollars a day, and as with the PHS medical offices, the patient would receive free care if he or she did not have the money with which to pay even this modest amount. Every hospital patient would have a small, private room, each with its own bath.

The emphasis would be on quick, quality care, with ambulatory patients eating, at their expense, in a hospital cafeteria; meals for bedridden patients would be delivered to their rooms. (Meals would be free if the patient was without funds.)

PHS Academy students would not pay the costs of their medical education; instead, for each year of free training, they would serve one year on active duty as a doctor with the PHS. I am assuming that about 500 new PHS doctors a year would be trained in the PHS Academy, so as soon as the newly-trained PHS doctors finished their schooling, it would be possible for the PHS to open hundreds of additional PHS offices, staffed by the newly-trained doctors.

Thus, from a modest beginning with about 200 PHS offices, the PHS would continue to expand as more PHS-trained doctors became available. PHS nurses also would be needed, and I am assuming that the PHS Academy would also train nurses for the PHS.

Patients at a PHS office would not have a choice of physician. They would not have appointments. They would simply walk in, wait their turn, and see a doctor. If they needed emergency care, they would go next door to the hospital emergency room; if they went to the hospital ER first and did not need ER services, they would be sent next door to the PHS office.

Patients who had health insurance could choose whether to receive paid care in a regular doctor's office, for which their health insurance would pay, or in a PHS office, which they would pay for, out of their own pockets, at a cost of ten dollars per visit.

Most patients with health insurance probably would choose to go to a regular doctor's office, where they would have a choice of physician, where they could be seen on an appointment basis, and so on. My proposal is intended to have very little effect on the type of medical care that people who can afford health insurance receive today.

What I have said so far is with the assumption that most people who don't have health insurance, today, don't have it because they can't afford it, or they *think* they can't afford it. Some people simply gamble on not having big medical bills. If they then run into medical bills that they can't pay themselves, they don't have health insurance to defray big medical bills, and they lose their gamble. But some people don't have health insurance because they can't get it, for one reason or another, such as having been turned down because of pre-existing conditions.

Regardless of their reason(s) for not having health insurance, their lack of insurance means that, as a practical matter, they don't have a ticket of admission to the U. S. medical care system. My proposal gives *all* U. S. residents a ticket of admission, through the PHS, to the U. S. medical care system, just as if they had health insurance. And this ticket includes access to medical specialists of all kinds, and to hospital care.

Eventually, the PHS Academy, with its huge teaching hospital, will turn out medical specialists for the PHS. But at first, during a transitional period, it will be the function of the PHS doctors to act as gatekeepers to the existing medical specialists, with the U. S. government footing most of the bill. To keep costs down, however, the U. S. government will expect, and get, some price concessions. Here's the justification:

One reason that hospitals, now, charge so much is that they are charging you who have insurance extra, in order to make up for the losses they have to take, in order to care for people who don't have health insurance. By paying these costs, the government can then insist that hospital charges be reduced. And this will also have the effect of reducing the inflated prices that insurance companies have to pay that are then passed along to you, if you have health insurance. Thus, the costs for specialty care, and hospital care, can actually be much less than might at first appear to be the case.

The PHS medical care will be low cost but good; it will not include the deluxe features that we would all like to have, such as choice of physician, seeing doctors on an appointment basis, etc. The PHS care may be a bit spartan, but it will not, in any real sense, be inferior.

Most people will be happy to pay the nominal charges for the PHS services. And those who simply don't have the money won't have to pay. Technically, those who don't have the money and don't pay will still owe those nominal charges, so if they have income tax refunds coming, at any time in the future, what they owe will be deducted from their income tax refunds. But that's as much of a collection effort as my proposal contemplates; there would be no other efforts made by the government to collect. My proposal assumes that most people are honest, and will pay if they can.

The important thing about my proposal is that all U. S. residents who need medical care will get it, regardless of whether they have health insurance or not. They will not be given free insurance, and they will not be forced to buy insurance; in fact, my proposal would bar anyone from trying to force a U. S. resident to buy insurance.

Does my proposal amount to "socialized medicine?" No. It simply means that medical care will be available to any U. S. resident. It will be the medical care available through the PHS. It will not involve any long delays the way some national health plans, such as Canada's, seems to do. My proposal contemplates speedy, streamlined, efficient, low cost medical care.

The U. S. PHS is an existing organization, with two centuries of experience. It is a known quantity. I simply propose to expand it, and give it an expanded mission. It should have minimal effect on existing health insurance and on existing medical facilities and personnel. It is not intended to replace anything or anyone. It is simply aimed at giving U. S. residents who do not have health insurance the benefits of good medical care, at an affordable cost or, if necessary, at practically no cost at all. There will probably be some people who abuse the system. I say we accept that possibility, in order to make sure that the vast majority can benefit.

The PHS itself is non-political, and you don't see anyone from the PHS proposing its expansion. Nevertheless, I suggest that this is the most practical means of solving the health insurance crisis. The way to solve it is *not* by trying to do away with the existing health insurance system, or by trying to set up a "single payer" plan, or by doing any other radical reordering of health insurance, which is doing a generally fine job of taking care of the people who are fortunate enough to have it. But we must ask: what is the point here? Is it to give everyone health insurance? Or, is it to make good medical care available to those *without* health insurance?

I suggest it is the latter, and therefore, I invite your support for the proposal I have here outlined, a proposal which I believe could be implemented quickly, and at reasonable cost to all of us.

NOTE: I do not mean to suggest that the proposed PHS medical care system will be self-supporting; on the other hand, the revenue generated per hour by a PHS physician will go a long way toward supporting that physician. Remember that this will be a very streamlined operation, with no billing clerks, nothing paid to credit card companies, no costs for dealing with health insurance, no appointment clerks, etc. Medical records are all on computer, and the doctor or nurse simply enters what was done in updating the patient's medical record card. The PHS physicians will be able to see a very large number of patients per day. I am sure that there will be a need for some general tax revenue to support the system, but you should be aware of the fact that the PHS medical care system described here will undoubtedly function to keep down other medical care costs and thus will help keep down the cost of health insurance for those covered by health insurance. Do not believe any skeptic who claims that the PHS medical care system here proposed will be ghastly expensive. Also, I want to clarify a few points: 1) It may be necessary to substitute some higher figure, such as $15 or even $20, at points in this article where I have used the figure of $10; 2) I assume that the PHS system described would take care of any U. S. resident who needs medical care. 3) I don't believe the availability of medical services through the PHS should be means-tested; others may disagree with me but that's where I stand on this point. And one more thing: I am very serious when I suggest that the cost of medical services generally should come down with the advent of the PHS expansion that I propose here.

NUMBER TEN:

TERM LIMITS FOR CONGRESS

No person shall be eligible to serve in one House of the Congress for more than twelve consecutive years. A break of at least two years is required to restore eligibility.

But this article of amendment shall not apply to any person currently serving in that House, nor shall service of an unexpired term, to which any person has been appointed or elected, be counted as part of the twelve years of service for purposes of this article.

Term Limits for Congress

I ran for the U. S. House of Representatives in 1992 and got about 94,000 votes. I raised, and spent, about $1,000. Actually, I spent a whole lot more than that, out of my own pocket, and also about a year of my life, and got nothing for it, except a lot of interesting experiences.

My opponent was a 34-year incumbent. He had about $500,000 in his campaign account at the start of his campaign for reelection that year, and after his re-election, again, he probably had about the same amount in the bank. He got about 158,000 votes, as I recall.

But two years later, he got beat, by a man who was able to spend about $650,000 out of his own pocket, plus what he was able to raise, who looked at what I had done with my paltry resources and realized that my opponent was vulnerable to someone who could buy enough media attention to overcome the enormous advantages of incumbency.

Frankly, it is the advantages of incumbency, with all that goes with it, such as seniority, chairmanship of important congressional committees or subcommittees, plus the ability to help direct financial advantages to the home state or district, in addition to being able to vote oneself generous pay increases, that make it very difficult for any challenger to make much headway against a well-entrenched Congress person or senator.

Incumbents of any political persuasion have such an advantage, going into any campaign for re-election, that they are able to attract campaign contributions almost without limit. Indeed, efforts to put limits on political contributions are almost ridiculous because the beneficiaries of those contributions write the campaign finance laws, and needless to say, they write the laws in such a way as to be gotten around, usually rather easily. Time and again, reformers have patted themselves (usually very publicly) on the back, only to see their efforts go for naught, often in the very next election cycle, when--surprise, surprise--the incumbents win again!

Incumbency carries some real advantages for the political system; mostly, these advantages are in terms of experience and continuity. I am here referring especially to the fact that, in order to accomplish many things, time is required.

But challengers often bring new ideas, and new insights, into the political system, and to the extent that incumbency hinders the entry of such new ideas and new insights, the system suffers. A balance needs to be struck, and right now, the system is badly out of whack because the incumbents are so overwhelmingly favored.

Take my case, for example. My new ideas were in the realm of reform, particularly with regard to deficit spending by the federal government; I had figured out how to effectively cure the problem of deficit spending, and it was obvious to me that my know-how was needed.

But I didn't get elected. I gave my new ideas to the man who was elected two years later, but obviously, he didn't use them. Unfortunately, this is what usually happens with such ideas. A few months ago, for example, I gave my ideas to a Congress person who was on the verge of leaving the U. S. House, to run for another office (he lost). He would have had time to do something with them--but he didn't.

The point I'm making is that the system needs new ideas, and often doesn't get them. Congressional challengers win only about five per cent of the time. Which means that incumbents win about ninety-five per cent of the time, and that is truly unfortunate, because the consequence is, most of the time, that new ideas don't penetrate the walls of the political system; thus, the people the system is supposed to serve, suffer.

Various reform ideas have surfaced from time to time. One such idea is that of public financing for political campaigns. The idea is that some challengers might get elected if they have some financial help. But they usually are given a lot of hoops to jump through, and these hoops usually interfere with, rather than help, the candidates they are supposed to help.

My impression is that public financing is an ineffective, and rarely successful, means of bringing new ideas into the political system. It gives proponents of public financing schemes something to feel good about, but that is about all that it accomplishes.

The best way of dealing with incumbents is to give them a reasonable time to accomplish something, and then to force them out, opening the way for new blood, and new ideas, to come into the political system.

Thus, the best way of dealing with incumbents is through term limits. Frankly, it is not only the best way, it is the *only* way of *effectively* solving the incumbency problem, in all of its dimensions. For example, take the matter of seniority. If all members of the House, or the Senate, are limited to the same number of years in office, there is little basis for the seniority system that has plagued Congress almost from the beginning.

Committees were not foreseen as a problem by the Framers of the Constitution, who used committees, effectively, during the drafting of the Constitution themselves. However, those were *temporary* committees; it is the day-in-day-out *standing* committees of Congress that have been the problem.

Here's an example of the problem: a certain chairman, with a lot of seniority, "bottles up" a certain bill that has substantial support in Congress and undoubtedly would be passed into law promptly; but the chairman doesn't like the bill--or he has "friends" who will pay him a lot of money [or give him substantial campaign contributions]--if he will just keep on blocking that bill, keep it from becoming law. Is this bribery, which is against the law? Certainly, but it's not *called* bribery, and Congress people do this, and get away with it, all the time. If term limits require, as a practical matter, that committee chairmanships rotate from time to time, then the possibilities for the type of corruption that I just illustrated will largely go away.

The type of term limits that I favor would be somewhat similar to the type that Congress itself imposed on presidents, by means of the 22nd Amendment to the U. S. Constitution, proposed by Congress in March of 1947 and ratified, by the state legislatures, nearly four years later, in 1951.

For those unfamiliar with the background of the 22nd Amendment, a little history lesson: The U. S. Constitution, as originally written, contained no mention of term limits at all, even though the idea of limiting terms or limiting re-election possibilities for officeholders had been discussed, at various times, by the delegates to the Constitutional Convention of 1787. George Washington, the first president, had served two four-year terms, but had then rather publicly declined to serve longer. The precedent he thus set became the practical limit on presidential terms for more than 14 decades. Although his cousin, President Theodore Roosevelt, had run for what would have been almost a third term, it was President Franklin D. Roosevelt who actually broke Washington's two term tradition, seeking, and winning, a third full term in 1940, and then being elected to a fourth term in 1944, of which FDR actually served less than three months before dying in office, in April of 1945.

Although FDR was greatly honored for his long and distinguished service as president of the United States, the only elective federal office he ever held, it was due to a vast consensus that he had served too long that Congress, in March, 1947, less than two years after his death, officially proposed, by a two-thirds vote in both the House and the Senate, what became the 22nd Amendment to the U. S. Constitution, what many people saw as the anti-FDR amendment. I'm going to quote the text of the 22nd Amendment here:

> No person shall be elected to the office of the President more than twice, and no person who has held the office of President, or acted as President, for more than two years of a term to which some other person was elected President shall be elected to the office of the President more than once.
>
> But this article shall not apply to any person holding the office of President when this article was proposed by the Congress, and shall not prevent any person who may be holding the office of President, or acting as President, during the term within which this article becomes operative from holding the office of President or acting as President during the remainder of such term.

The 22nd Amendment was ratified in February, 1951. The second paragraph, in essence, exempted President Truman from the operation of the 22nd Amendment. One of the interesting aspects of the 22nd Amendment was that it amounted to a lifetime disqualification for a person who had already served two terms as president; it would have affected the situations of both Presidents Roosevelt (but of course, both were dead by the time the 22nd Amendment went into effect).

In 1992, when I was running for Congress, there was a strong reform tide running, and a key reform being widely proposed was that of term limits for Congress. There were several organizations promoting term limits, some of them also promoting term limits for other elective offices besides Congress. I recall signing term limits pledges sponsored by several different organizations.

In general, the term limits organizations seemed to me very reluctant to try to accomplish term limits through constitutional amendment. This appeared to me to be wishful thinking. I thought then, and still feel, that term limits *for*

Congress can be accomplished *only* through an amendment to the U. S. Constitution, and I was not at all surprised that the U. S. Supreme Court, some time after 1992, so ruled.

During the 1994 election cycle, term limits were still very much an issue, and the Contract with America, sponsored by a Republican organization, GOPAC, which led to the election of a Republican majority in the U. S. House of Representatives for the first time in several decades, included a term limits pledge.

However, term limits was the one pledge made, in the Contract with America, which the Republican-dominated Congress did not redeem, much to my disappointment. Furthermore, Congress persons of both parties, in some cases, reneged on term limits pledges that they had made to their supporters. And on the other hand, some Congress persons *did* abide by their term limits pledges, even though there was no enforcement mechanism except for the ballot box, which wasn't always effective.

As the years rolled on, the reform movement generally, and the term limits movement specifically, petered out. In my efforts to revive it, I recognize that there is little current interest in term limits, even though I believe that term limits are needed, now more than ever. The voters, in the 2006 election cycle, punished the Republicans by throwing quite a number of them out of office, and this happened in both the Senate and the House of Representatives. Democrats took control of both houses of Congress. The war in Iraq obviously had something to do with the change in leadership, but so did scandals that, in some instances, involved Republicans; also, a large cause of the unrest with Republican candidates involved voter disappointment with the recent performance of Republican members, and this was especially true with respect to the House.

Since the 22nd Amendment obviously meant a vacancy in the White House, to be filled in the 2008 election cycle, a large field of candidates seeking both Republican and Democratic presidential nominations, dominated the political news for many months, crowding out any efforts by congressional candidates to win media attention. At some point, however, congressional candidates, including both incumbents and challengers, had to come forth; talk of term limits was largely absent, because there were so many other important issues to talk about.

However, term limits for members of Congress are needed, now more than ever. Reason: the voters are obviously disgusted with Congress, and approval ratings, according to recent published polls, have been running at about ten per cent.

The voters, as a group, are disgusted with Congress for good reason; incumbency is largely to blame. Congress is widely seen as out of touch and ineffective, in need of the new blood and new ideas that could be provided by challengers, who nevertheless face funding problems that are larger than ever. Money is available, but the voters are increasingly suspicious about members of Congress being for sale, and that suspicion, unfortunately, has a factual basis. I suggest that term limits for Congress may be an idea, the time for which has come.

I'm sure you'll observe the similarity between my term limits amendment proposal and the 22nd Amendment that applies only to the president. My proposal is meant to do just one simple thing: break up the lengthy incumbencies. The second paragraph is important in order to persuade Congress to officially propose this as an amendment to the U. S. Constitution. A constitutional convention called pursuant to Article V of the Constitution would not need to include this language and could make the amendment effective much sooner, but for obvious, practical reasons, Congress is not going to allow a constitutional convention for purposes of officially proposing a term limits amendment. It is unfortunate, but probably true, that term limits for Congress are going to take a long time to accomplish; all the more reason for early action. I want to make it very clear how this term limits amendment to the U. S. Constitution would work. The overall limit is 12 consecutive years in one House of Congress; that means six two-year terms in the U. S. House of Representatives, OR two six-year terms in the U. S. Senate. After six two-year terms in the House, for example, a person could do any number of other things (run for governor, or the State legislature, or the U. S. Senate, or some other office) and then, after a two-year break, if the former Congress person so desired, he or she could run for the House again, and if elected again, could serve as many as six more two-year terms in the House. It's important to note that, unlike the 22nd Amendment that applies to presidents, my term limits amendment does not permanently bar a Congress person from serving more than 12 years in one House of Congress; after a two-year break, if the voters want a particular Congress person back, they can have their way, and he/she can serve up to another 12 consecutive years.

Also, members of either House of Congress at the time the term limits amendment was adopted would be exempt; it would only apply to people elected later. And service of partial terms would not be counted. These provisions are intended to give Congress persons no excuse for not helping to get the term limits amendment adopted, since they themselves would not be affected by it. I'm well aware of the fact that it would take many years for the term limits amendment to become fully effective in breaking up the long-term incumbencies; we need to get started, now!

I know that some people will argue that there is no need for a limit on congressional terms. Here is my reply to that line of argument:

1. There is no indication that the Founding Fathers ever intended to create a permanent governing class.

2. There is every indication that the present system is a failure; it has led to corruption, and worse; the low approval ratings for Congress ought to convince anyone that something is seriously wrong.

Finally, I would note that the 22nd Amendment has not been repealed; it's been on the books since 1951, and in more than 50 years, there has been no serious effort to repeal it. Clearly, reasonable term limits for members of Congress is a long-overdue reform. The voters obviously agree; a poll taken in January of 2013 showed overwhelming public support for congressional term limits. The poll showed 75 per cent of adults favored term limits.

NUMBER ELEVEN:

AMENDING, TO AMEND

Conventions called by the Congress pursuant to Article V on the applications of the legislatures of the several States shall be limited to consideration of proposed amendments fairly within the ambit of such applications unless such applications clearly specify that the Convention sought is to be without limitation. Congress shall publish, at least annually, the details of all of such applications that are pending. All of such applications shall be considered pending for a period of ten years from the date of submission to the Congress, unless a particular application shall specify an earlier expiration.

Amending, to Amend: Restoring the Original Intent of the Founding Fathers

On Monday, August 6, 1787, the Constitutional Convention, meeting in Philadelphia, heard from the Committee of Detail.

The Convention had been adjourned for eleven days on Thursday, July 26th, to give a five-man committee an opportunity to take the 23 resolutions so far approved and try to turn them into what George Washington called some "method and form." Secrecy still prevailed, but many outside the hall were clamoring for information about what was going on. The delegates themselves needed some sort of inventory of what they had done toward drafting what they hoped would be a plan for a more effective government.

Members of the Committee of Detail were: Edmund Randolph of Virginia, who actually wrote the draft submitted by the Committee;

James Wilson of Pennsylvania, who polished it; Nathaniel Gorham of Massachusetts and Oliver Ellsworth of Connecticut who served on the Committee; and John Rutledge of South Carolina, Chairman of the Committee of Detail.

While the Committee of Detail was working to organize the work that the Convention had done up to this point, the other delegates scattered. George Washington, the presiding officer, went trout fishing with friends. One of the friends was Gouverneur Morris, delegate from Pennsylvania, who within a few weeks would be the man who, almost single-handedly, would write the final draft of what we know as the United States Constitution.

On this trip, while Morris was fishing, Washington rode over to Valley Forge, Pennsylvania, to visit what he called "The old Cantonment" occupied by his army during the winters of 1777 and 1778; he noted that the site was already in ruins, and that part of it was under cultivation.

But back to Philadelphia, on Monday, August 6th. The Committee of Detail had not attempted to furnish a proposed draft of the Constitution.

The members of the Committee directed the printer to make just enough copies of their report so that each of the delegates would have one.

The Committee of Detail draft consisted of 23 numbered Articles. I want to refer, at this point, to Article XIX:

> On the application of the Legislatures of two thirds of the States in the Union, for an amendment of this Constitution, the Legislature of the United States shall call a Convention for that purpose.

It is thus clear, beyond any doubt, that the *original intent* of the delegates to the Constitutional Convention of 1787 was that the *state* legislatures (that is, two-thirds of them) would ask (apply to) *Congress* to call a *Convention* for the purpose of amending the Constitution. To put it another way, the delegates to the Constitutional Convention of 1787 had in mind a meeting similar to the one that they were then having, for the purpose of *amending* the Constitution. They were not thinking about having Congress itself do the amending. In fact, they themselves were deliberately avoiding Congress, as it was at that time. As they saw it, the only role that Congress was to have in *amending* the Constitution was to *call a Convention.* The Convention would do the actual amending. It is very important to understand this point, in the light of what has happened since the Convention of 1787.

Having resumed work on Monday, August 6th, the Constitutional Convention then began the final weeks of work on the new plan of government, using the 23 articles of the report from the Committee of Detail (sometimes referred to as the "First Draft" of the Constitution) as the basis for discussion. Several weeks later, the Convention adjourned again, this time for only four days. On September 10th, an entirely new Committee, called the Committee of Style, was given the job of putting the Constitution into final form.

Members of the Committee of Style were: James Madison of Virginia, Alexander Hamilton of New York, Rufus King of Massachusetts, and Gouverneur Morris of Pennsylvania, with William Samuel Johnson of Connecticut as chairman. Morris did most of the actual drafting of the final version, which was then (with minor changes) approved and then ordered "engrossed" and brought in for signature on September 17th, when final remarks were made, the document was signed by most of those still present, and the Convention then adjourned to the City Tavern for a final meal before the delegates scattered, heading for home and, they hoped, ratification of the Constitution.

Which happened, then, sometimes quickly, and sometimes only after great struggles had ensued.

The new government got underway in early 1789 with eleven of the original thirteen States aboard; North Carolina joined later that year, and Rhode Island followed in 1790.

The last State to ratify before the new government got underway was New York, and it was during the ratification struggle there (actually the question was not really ratification because ten States had already ratified and only nine were needed) that 85 "letters" signed by Publius were published in New York City newspapers. Publius was the pseudonym for the three actual authors (James Madison, Alexander Hamilton, and John Jay), whose identity was revealed years later, with the 85 letters published in book form as *The Federalist Papers.*

The focus of my paper is on Article V of the U. S. Constitution, and the subject is the procedure for amending the U. S. Constitution, as it was finally approved and ratified, and as it still stands, today. I quoted above the original intent of the delegates to the Constitutional Convention of 1787, as set forth in the "First Draft," that is, in Article XIX of the report by the Committee of Detail.

Now, here is Article V of the U. S. Constitution, in pertinent part:

> The Congress, whenever two thirds of both Houses shall deem it necessary, shall propose Amendments to this Constitution, or, on the Application of the Legislatures of two thirds of the several States, shall call a Convention for proposing Amendments, which, in either Case, shall be valid to all Intents and Purposes, as Part of this Constitution, when ratified by the Legislatures of three fourths of the several States, or

> by Conventions in three fourths thereof, as the one or the other Mode of Ratification may be proposed by the Congress; . . .

You may well ask: where did all this come from? The delegates to the Constitutional Convention obviously realized that the new bicameral legislature that they were planning would be quite different from the Congress that they were then avoiding; and they also realized that the new Congress would be in session every year. Therefore, they would give the new Congress *itself* the power to propose amendments to the Constitution, as well as the power to call a Convention for the purpose of proposing amendments when requested to do so by the legislatures of two-thirds of the states, which had been the original idea, as set forth in Article XIX of the Committee of Detail report.

In either case, a proposed amendment would not become a part of the Constitution *until it had been ratified.* And here was where the delegates to the Constitutional Convention focused their attention. Articles XXI, XXII, and XXIII of the Committee of Detail report were concerned with the question of how the new Constitution itself was to be ratified, and put into effect. Obviously, this was a matter of great concern to them, and in the final analysis, they came up with something very simple, as compared with the very involved procedure (and which *did* involve the Congress as it was at that time) that they had been thinking about, some weeks earlier. Here is the pertinent part of Article VII of the U. S. Constitution, as they finally approved it:

> The Ratification of the Conventions of nine States, shall be sufficient for the Establishment of this Constitution between the States so ratifying the Same.

This is the key to understanding the *amendment* procedure that the delegates to the Constitutional Convention of 1787 finally decided upon. They decided that a positive vote by the Legislatures of three-fourths of the States, or by Conventions in three-fourths of the States, would be needed to *ratify* a proposed Constitutional amendment, whereupon the amendment, for all intents and purposes, would be considered to be a part of the U. S. Constitution.

And here it is useful to read Alexander Hamilton's explanation of the amendment procedure, as he set it forth in Federalist No. 85. Notice that he totally ignores the fact that Article V, as finally adopted, gives *Congress* the power to *propose* Constitutional amendments. His focus is on the original intent expressed in Article XIX of the Committee of Detail report:

> By the fifth article of the plan, the Congress will be *obliged* "on the application of the legislatures of two thirds of the States [which at present amount to nine] to call a convention for proposing amendments which *shall be valid*, to all intents and purposes, as part of the Constitution, when ratified by the legislatures of three fourths of the States, or by conventions in three fourths thereof." The words of this article are peremptory. The Congress "*shall* call a convention." Nothing in this particular is left to the discretion of that body. . . . [Italics in the original.]

What has actually happened is that Congress has totally monopolized the process of amending the

U. S. Constitution. At no time since the Constitution was first ratified, in 1789, has there ever been a Convention called, for the purpose of proposing Constitutional amendments, at the request of two-thirds of the State legislatures. Many of the state legislatures have asked Congress to call a Constitutional Convention. . . many, many times.

Why, then, has there never been such a Constitutional Convention? Why has what Alexander Hamilton *said* would happen, *never* happened?

The answer is, to put it rather bluntly, that Congress has failed to facilitate Convention applications from the State legislatures, in order to continue its monopoly power over the constitutional amendment process.

Here's what has been going on. Remember, it takes "applications" from the legislatures of two-thirds of the States before Congress is "obligated" to call a Constitutional Convention. Let's say the legislature of your State passes a resolution asking Congress to call a Constitutional Convention for the purpose of, say, proposing an amendment to require the

Federal government to balance its budget. (Hint: this *has* happened, literally *dozens* of times, in fact.)

In other words, the majority of your State's legislators want to stop the U. S. Congress from engaging in deficit spending. They want to cancel Uncle Sam's credit card! And across the country, there are similar resolutions being passed in other State legislatures. The resolutions are sent to Congress. Here they are filed away, and more or less forgotten. No one in Congress pays much attention to them.

We now have 50 States. It takes resolutions ("applications") from 34 State legislatures (two-thirds of 50 is 34, rounded off). Who's counting? Congress, certainly, is *not* counting!

The ordinary citizen of the U. S. may be in favor of a Constitutional Convention that would consider amendment proposals of a particular type, such as requiring the federal government to stop deficit spending, but they want to limit a Constitutional Convention so that it can't propose amendments on any other topic. (Never mind the fact that Congress can propose amendments of almost any kind, any day Congress is in session.)

What happens, therefore, is that your State legislature asks Congress to call a Constitutional Convention for the purpose of proposing amendments of a particular kind. The legislature of another State passes a resolution asking Congress to call a Constitutional Convention for proposing amendments of some other kind. Some of the States put time limits in their resolutions, declaring them null and void if not acted upon by a particular date.

Congress gets these resolutions all the time. They are just received and filed away. No one keeps track of them or tries to coordinate them. Congress has absolutely no interest in keeping track of them or in coordinating them. Why? Because Congress has a vested interest in maintaining its control over the amendment process.

Look at it this way: if citizens succeed in getting a "balanced budget" constitutional amendment that really works, the Congressional "credit card" goes away, and with it, the power of your Congress person or senator to spend your tax money on projects for which he/she can then claim credit. It's all about power, and Congress is afraid of losing it, if you interfere by means of a constitutional amendment.

Actually, some members of Congress deliberately use "scare" tactics to try to frighten citizens, and discourage them from trying to get a Constitutional Convention. For example, they may claim that there is a danger of a "runaway" Constitutional Convention, which is nonsense. If all that a Constitutional Convention can do is *propose* amendments, what's the harm in that? Any proposed amendment requires ratification, which requires a positive vote by three-fourths of the State legislatures, or a positive vote by three-fourths of special State ratification conventions. Without ratification, a proposed constitutional amendment simply dies, something that has happened any number of times.

With 50 states, it takes 38 states (three-fourths of 50, rounded off) to ratify. Remember the so-called Equal Rights Amendment (ERA)? A lot of feminists do. In that case, Congress proposed the ERA and sent it out to the State legislatures for ratification. After the legislatures of 35 States had voted for ratification, a storm of opposition suddenly arose. Not one of the remaining 15 State legislatures voted to ratify (three more were needed), so the ERA died.

Actually, it is fairly easy to kill a proposed constitutional amendment. Forty-nine of the 50 State legislatures are bicameral; that is, they have two chambers, often a house and a senate, but terminology varies from state to state. Opponents of a proposed amendment to the U. S. Constitution only have to get one chamber in each of 13 State legislatures to vote it down. Proponents have to get a *positive* vote in *both* chambers of 38 State legislatures in order to get a proposed U. S. constitutional amendment ratified.

By now, you should realize that what I say is true: Congress has been monopolizing the constitutional amendment process, contrary to the intent of those who wrote the Constitution at the Philadelphia Convention in 1787. If you read Article V, you see that the Philadelphia Convention delegates intended for there to be four possible combinations by which constitutional amendments could be proposed, and ratified. Of the four possible combinations, two have *never* been used. A third combination has been used once; that was in the early 1930s, when Congress proposed Amendment XXI, which would repeal the XVIII (prohibition) Amendment, and sent it out to special State ratification conventions rather than to the State legislatures, where "drys" would have been able to easily defeat it (see above).

In all other cases, Congress has proposed the amendments and sent them to the State legislatures for ratification. We have had 27 amendments to the U. S. Constitution since 1789; 26 out of the 27 have been approved using this procedure. In fact, if you ask your senators or your Congress person, they will probably tell you that this is the normal way to amend the Constitution, and any other procedure is odd, which is exactly opposite to the intent of the delegates to the 1787 Constitutional Convention, as I have here demonstrated.

The truth is that Congress, for better or worse, has in essence taken away from the citizens their rights to participate in the constitutional amendment process. Is there a way that citizens can get their rights back? The answer is yes, and I'm going to spell it out for you, now. We, the people, need to work to get Congress to "propose" the constitutional amendment I have proposed here, and send it out to the States for ratification. This amendment will restore your right to participate in the constitutional amendment process:

1. It will clarify, not change, Article V.

2. It will require Congress to round up, and publicize, the various applications for a Constitutional Convention that have already been submitted by the State legislatures, as well as those that are submitted in the future.

I put in the ten year period so that Congress does not have to keep track of, and publicize, old Convention applications that are no longer of interest to anyone. I put in the limitation language in order to make it clear, beyond any doubt, that fears of a "runaway" Constitutional Convention are totally groundless.

I want to stress here the point that there should be *no* hesitation by any senator or Congress person about working to get this proposed amendment adopted--unless such senator or Congress person intends to help continue the monopoly that Congress now maintains over the constitutional amendment process. In which case, it is obvious that *you* should go to work to *defeat* that senator or Congress person when he/she is up for election!

It is also obvious that this is a totally nonpartisan proposal. Democrat, Republican, whatever, it doesn't matter. *You* are just trying to get *your* rights restored to what the Framers of the Constitution intended! Don't let anyone try to convince you otherwise! As the title of this article suggests, this is clearly a case of *Amending* . . . in order *To Amend*, so that *you* can participate in the constitutional amendment process, possibly even as a delegate to a future Constitutional Convention, which is exactly what the Founding Fathers intended when they wrote the U. S. Constitution in 1787.

NUMBER TWELVE:

CONGRESSIONAL RULES

1. Neither House of Congress shall establish or maintain any rule or custom that permits or requires consideration of any matter of business to be delayed for a period of more than 24 hours. A simple majority shall decide all questions unless the Constitution requires otherwise.

2. All members of Congress shall maintain one or more offices in the District or State from which the member was elected.

3. Either House of Congress may permit its members to vote on matters of routine business from their offices in their respective Home Districts or States, as long as their votes can be, and are, tallied and recorded instantaneously, and as long as they can communicate with each other instantaneously. All votes in both Houses shall be cast by the

members only, and shall be both public and recorded.

4. The presiding officers of each House shall communicate with each other, from time to time, and shall, by common agreement, designate those matters of business that are not routine and call for the members to assemble at the nation's capital, or at some other place within the contiguous continental States, for the conduct of business not considered routine.

5. If the presiding officers cannot agree as to which matters of business are to be considered other than routine, they shall cause the members to vote thereon.

6. All regular bills, including budget bills and appropriations bills, and all proposed amendments to the Constitution, shall be voted upon, during the session in which they were introduced, regardless of any committee action, provided, however, that in order to qualify for this mandatory vote, the bill or proposal must have the signed endorsement of at least ten per cent of the membership of the House or the Senate, respectively, including

the endorsement of at least four members from States which are not contiguous to the State of the member who first introduced the bill or proposal. If at least twenty per cent of the membership of the particular House vote in favor in the first mandatory vote, the bill or proposal shall receive a second mandatory vote at least seven days following the first mandatory vote. No member shall compensate another member, in any manner whatsoever, in order to obtain the endorsement or favorable vote of the other member with respect to a mandatory vote pursuant to this provision. No more than two mandatory votes need be taken with respect to any particular bill or proposal, and the ordinary rules shall apply thereto.

Modernizing Congress

Members of the general public look on in frustration as the U. S. Senate fails, time and again, to act on important public questions in a timely manner. Reading of the U. S. Constitution provides no hint that the Founding Fathers ever dreamed of the senate's filibuster rules that allow one Senator to delay action through endless "debate," which may involve nothing more than reading something totally irrelevant to the business at hand, aloud.

At the present time, 60 votes are required to cut off debate, and it is rare that one side commands 60 votes, which means that a minority can keep the U. S. Senate from conducting its business.

This has got to stop. My twelfth proposed constitutional amendment will stop such nonsense, forever. Twenty-four hours would be the delay limitation, and a simple majority vote would decide the fate of all bills, unless the Constitution required otherwise.

Also, this is a large country. Washington, D. C. is on the east coast, many hours away from the home of a Congress person who may live thousands of miles away. My amendment proposal would permit members to vote on routine matters from the offices they must maintain in their home States or House Districts.

Another reform in this proposed amendment would require mandatory up-or-down votes on important bills or proposals, regardless of committee action or other delaying devices.

With these reforms in place, it's just possible that public approval of what Congress is doing might improve.

SECTION TWO

The Five Additional (draft) Amendment Proposals, Presented for Purposes of Discussion

NUMBER THIRTEEN:

FINANCING FEDERAL ELECTION CAMPAIGNS

No one, except a natural person who is a legal resident of the United States, shall be permitted to contribute to a candidate, or organization, of a person who is seeking election or re-election to a national political office, *to wit,* to the office of President or Vice

President, or to the office of member of the United States Senate or to the office of member of the United States House of Representatives. All contributions from ineligible contributors shall be returned to the contributor(s) if possible, and if not possible, shall be turned over to the Treasurer of the United States and treated as a part of the general funds of the United States. Any such candidate shall be permitted to contribute to his or her own candidacy without limit. All eligible natural persons shall be permitted to contribute to any other candidate within limits expressed herein, but the contributions of all such persons to any individual candidate that exceed $1,000 at any point within any one calender year shall promptly be reported by or on behalf of said candidate(s) to the Treasurer of the United States, who shall make public all of such disclosures on a quarterly basis. Annual contributions from any one such person that exceed one-quarter of the current base annual salary of the office which the candidate for election is seeking shall be promptly returned to the contributor, if possible, and if not possible, shall be paid over to the Treasurer and treated as part of the general funds of the United States.

Any organization or natural person may contribute funds to any organization for the publication or dissemination of ideas otherwise legal, in unlimited amount, but no such organization shall publicize the candidacy of any identifiable candidate for national political office, either directly or indirectly, regardless of whether that person is currently an actual candidate for national political office or not. Any violation of this paragraph shall subject the violator to total forfeiture of all funds belonging to the organization to the Treasurer as aforesaid. Such organizations shall file, with the Treasurer, annual reports of contributions received that exceed $10,000 from any one other organization or natural person, fully disclosing the identity and address of each contributor.

Nothing herein shall have any effect whatsoever on any effort by the United States government to provide for public financing of any Federal political candidates and campaigns.

Campaign Spending Limits, Revisited

In the 2012 presidential campaign, we got a chance to see what unlimited spending in a political campaign looked like, free of any meaningful restraints. This was the result of the Supreme Court's decision in *Citizens United,* and it was not pretty. In the end, we all were almost punch-drunk from the spending, which deluged us in TV commercials for political candidates, including commercials that were full of lies.

Past efforts to limit spending, by statute, such as McCain-Feingold, have been ineffective, precisely because they were easily circumvented and were violative of the First Amendment to the U. S. Constitution. There is only one way of bringing about some limitation to this madness: amend the constitution itself to spell out a reasonable set of rules. The proposed draft amendment, here, is submitted for purposes of discussion.

This proposed amendment does two things: it sets out the rules, and limits, for all Federal political campaigns, and it sets out the rules, and limits, that organizations, and corporations have to follow. It puts in some reasonable dollar limits, and it puts in the sanctions for violations. No one is threatened with prison. But violators lose funds to the U. S. Treasury if they don't behave. Organizations, such as corporations, are free to express their opinions, but they are not free to build up some person to be a future candidate. Corporations, and organizations such as unions, are not free to contribute money to candidates at all. Also, they cannot "publicize the candidacy" of identifiable candidates, which means that a union cannot mobilize its members to "get out the vote" for candidates the union favors; the sanction is total forfeiture of all of the organization's funds to the U. S. Treasury!

As a practical matter, the First Amendment rights of organizations are limited only very slightly; they can't talk up Federal political candidates, and they have to report large contributions. There remain the full, First Amendment rights of natural persons. Only when they are candidates for Federal office are there restrictions, and the restrictions are pretty much limited to reporting contributions. The annual amount that one individual can contribute is limited, but there are no other limits on what a candidate can collect from contributors who are "natural persons." The effort here is to keep one individual contributor from "buying" the candidate. Obviously, a candidate with a lot of rich friends is going to have a financial advantage over one who does not have a lot of rich friends, but that's always been the case.

Some degree of public financing of political candidates remains a viable option. The last paragraph of my amendment proposal is intended to make that clear. Thus, it will be possible to again use the income tax "checkoff" to partially fund presidential campaigns.

NUMBER FOURTEEN:

RESTRICTING MORTGAGE FORECLOSURES

A first mortgage on a homestead upon which the mortgagor(s) made regular payments for a period of five years or more shall henceforth not be subject to foreclosure but shall, instead, be considered a nonforeclosable lien. At the option of the mortgagor(s), the payment terms on such a mortgage shall be modified to an amount not exceeding a sum equal to no more than 25% of the mortgagor's gross income, for the lifetime of the mortgagor(s), even if this causes the balance due on the mortgage to become a negative amount. The total amount due on any and all mortgages on such homestead shall be subject to similar modification, at the option of the mortgagor(s) and for the lifetime of the mortgagor(s), so that the total payments of all mortgages on the said homestead shall not exceed 35% of the mortgagor's gross

income. A Federal Bankruptcy court having jurisdiction of the homestead property shall promptly enforce the provisions hereof by appropriate order(s), upon application, without the necessity of a petition in bankruptcy having been filed.

Some Security for Distressed Homeowners

It is fundamentally unfair for homeowners, having regularly paid their home mortage obligations for many years, to be faced with foreclosure caused by national economic conditions that were unforeseeable and beyond their ability to prevent.

In essence, they are being deprived of their property without due process of law, in violation of their constitutional property rights, by economic conditions beyond their control. They should not be the ones to suffer. They may have lost their jobs, again due to conditions beyond their control.

The purpose of my fourteenth draft amendment proposal is to make it possible for distressed homeowners, at their option, to halt foreclosure proceedings against them and to elect restructuring of their mortgage obligations so that they can stay in their homes for the rest of their days.

Thus, homeowners who have been making their mortgage payments for five years or longer cannot be foreclosed. Their mortgages are converted, by operation of law, to nonforecloseable liens.

All Federal bankruptcy Courts with jurisdiction over the property are given the duty, and the power, of enforcing this proposed amendment, without any necessity of an actual bankruptcy proceeding.

NUMBER FIFTEEN:

IMMIGRATION REFORM

From and after the date of ratification hereof, children born in the United States of America shall be considered citizens of the United States of America, and of the State in which they are born, provided that the mother of the child is either a citizen of the United States of America at the time the child is born or is in the process of becoming a naturalized citizen, or is married to the biological father of the child who is himself either a citizen of the United States of America at the time the child is born or is in the process of becoming a naturalized citizen. This Amendment shall be deemed to be a change in some past interpretations of the Fourteenth Amendment to the United States Constitution. The citizenship status of any child born in the United States prior to the ratification of this Amendment shall not, in any way, be changed by this Amendment. Congress shall have the

power to define, from time to time, by ordinary legislation, the meaning of the term "in the process of becoming a naturalized citizen," and no definition of this term, other than by Congress, shall have any validity whatsoever.

All persons who were born in the United States, or were brought to the United States at the age of six or less, and have attended school in the United States for ten years or more, and who have abided by the laws of the United States except for the immigration laws of the United States, and, notwithstanding the foregoing, be not otherwise already citizens of the United States, shall be considered to be "in the process of becoming a naturalized citizen," and shall become eligible to apply for a certificate of United States citizenship upon the attainment of the age of 18 years, with their applications, reasonably supported by documents and affidavits, making the factual showing required by this provision.

Ideas for Immigration Reform

We are told that we have twelve million illegal immigrants living among us. What to do with them?

Mitt Romney's idea that they should just deport themselves went over like a lead balloon.

My amendment proposal attempts to deal with two specific problems. The first paragraph is intended to deal with the "anchor baby" phenomenon. This where a pregnant female "illegal" gets herself to a U. S. hospital emergency room, whereupon she delivers a baby who immediately becomes a U. S. citizen, thanks to the Fourteenth Amendment to the U. S. Constitution, which says, in pertinent part, that "All persons born . . . in the United States, and subject to the jurisdiction thereof, are citizens of the United States and of any State wherein they reside." The newborn citizen infant then becomes the "anchor" which pulls the mother, and perhaps other relatives, into U. S. citizenship.

•

Not everyone agrees that the Fourteenth Amendment must be interpreted this way, but the "anchor baby" idea apparently has led to a lot of "illegals" being recognized as U. S. citizens. After all, a newborn infant needs its mother, doesn't it? You can't very well deport just the infant's mother, can you? And you certainly can't deport the child, who clearly becomes a citizen by being born in the U. S. A., according to the Fourteenth Amendment.

The first paragraph of my proposed amendment changes this. In order for the newborn child to be a U. S. citizen right off the bat, the mother must already be a U. S. citizen, or she must be "in the process of becoming a naturalized citizen" (the process is as defined by Congress) or she must be married to the biological father of the child, who is himself either a citizen or in the process of becoming a naturalized citizen. If the child does not become a citizen by being born to a parent who is already a citizen or is in the process of becoming a citizen, the child does not then serve as an "anchor baby."

Is this fair to the child? Yes. If the child does not automatically become a U. S. citizen just by being born in the U. S. A., the child then becomes a citizen of whatever country his birth parent is a citizen of, which is the same as being born in the home country.

The second paragraph sets out another path to U. S. citizenship for a child who does not automatically become a U. S. citizen by birth but who is either born in the U. S. or is brought to the U. S. on or before the child's sixth birthday. If this child then attends school in the U. S. for ten years or more and abides by U. S. laws (other than immigration laws), this child is considered to be in the process of becoming a U. S. citizen and upon reaching age 18, is eligible to apply for a certificate of U. S. citizenship.

This means that a child, who is born in the United States or is brought to the U. S. before age six and is attending school in the U. S. and is obeying U. S. laws, is considered to be in the process of becoming a U. S. citizen and cannot be deported, even though he or she has not yet attended school in the U. S. for ten years or more. But all the child has to do is stay in school for ten years or more, and stay out of trouble, and at age 18, the child is then eligible to apply for U. S. citizenship. By that time, the child has obviously learned English and absorbed U. S. culture, thus becoming eligible for U. S. citizenship, even though the child may have technically been an illegal immigrant to begin with. This is fair to the child, as well as being fair to the people of the U. S., whose immigration laws are being honored. The child, who may have technically violated the immigration laws by being brought into the U. S. (perhaps by parents), is not considered to be a violater if, and when, the child (or former child) applies for legal entry.

My proposed amendment does not solve all of our immigration problems but does solve many of them, and is fair, especially to the innocent children who may be involved.

On February 6, 2013, as I was working on some of the final details of this book, I saw on the Internet the story of Jose M., a perfect example of a person for whom my proposed amendment Number Fifteen would be made to order. Jose M. is an undocumented immigrant who says he "was brought to this country from Mexico when [he] was 2 years old."

Jose worked hard to get through school, including law school. But he's not a U. S. citizen. "I consider myself an American, and I want to play by the same rules as everyone else. But as it stands, I can never become a citizen. I can't adjust my status. For most of my life, I could have been arrested, detained, and deported."

Under the terms of my proposal Number Fifteen, Jose M. would be considered a person who is in the process of becoming a U. S. citizen. He's obviously met all the requirements and would be eligible to apply for a certificate of U. S. citizenship. So, all he needs is for my proposed amendment Number Fifteen to be formally proposed by Congress and ratified by the legislatures of 38 States.

NUMBER SIXTEEN:

LET THEM RUN

A member of the House or the Senate who is a candidate for President or Vice-President shall be permitted to run for re-election to that office while simultaneously running for President or Vice-President unless he or she cannot run for re-election to that office at that time because of a provision in the law pertaining to Term Limits.

Let Them Run, for Congress

Following the 2012 presidential election, it was announced that Representative Paul Ryan, who had just lost his bid for Vice-President as Mitt Romney's running mate, had won the election for his seat in the U. S. House of Representatives. Ryan had been a Congress person from the State of Wisconsin, and apparently, that State had permitted him to run for reelection to his House seat while at the same time running as Republican candidate for Vice-President.

Some States do not permit this, but all States should, and the purpose of this simple, proposed amendment to the U. S. Constitution is to make this possible in all of the States. There is no reason for members of the U. S. House of Representatives, or of the U. S. Senate, to be discouraged from running for President or Vice-President by making them give up their present positions in order to do so.

NUMBER SEVENTEEN:

NO FIRST USE OF NUCLEAR WEAPONS

Section 1. The United States of America shall not use nuclear or radioactive weapons against the people, territory, or armed forces of any other country, unless such other country shall have first used nuclear or radioactive weapons against the people, territory, or armed forces of the United States of America, or against the people, territory, or armed forces of a country which the United States is obligated by treaty to defend.

Section 2. Nothing contained herein shall be construed to prevent the United States of America from using nuclear or radioactive weapons to destroy weapons, or vehicles believed to contain weapons, which weapons are believed to be nuclear or radioactive, when such weapons or vehicles are in or over the territory of the United States of America,

or in or over any land area within approximately 100 nautical miles of the territory of the United States of America, or in or over any sea area within approximately 200 nautical miles of the territory of the United States of America, or in any area more than approximately 200 nautical miles above the earth. Nothing contained herein shall be construed to prevent the United States of America from using its nuclear weapons to defend the planet Earth from objects in space that appear to threaten the planet or any part thereof in any way, no matter the source thereof.

The Golden Rule, Applied to Nuclear Weapons

I first proposed this amendment to the U. S. Constitution in my 1986 book, *Great Restraint.* At that time, the "nuclear freeze" movement was in full swing, and I wrote that "a mutually verifiable nuclear freeze would require long and complex negotiations with the Soviet Union, if it could be brought into being at all."

A quarter of a century has passed, and today, the Soviet Union no longer exists, as such. The danger of a major nuclear war, as we perceived it 25 years ago, is not what we worry about now. Instead, our current concern is to keep Iran from developing nuclear weapons, with which to threaten the state of Israel.

It was, and is, my thought that a U. S. policy of "no first use" of nuclear weapons would allow us to discourage other nations from developing nuclear weapons. I saw this as extending the Biblical "Golden Rule" to nuclear weapons. We would keep our nuclear weapons, but we would legally forbid their use, in our Constitution, unless we or our treaty allies were attacked with nuclear weapons.

Any fool, of course, can easily come up with problems. Do we have to wait for an actual attack, or can we launch our weapons "on warning?" Certainly we do not want a nuclear "Pearl Harbor" to occur. How do we prevent such a thing from happening?

Also, it is difficult to think that adoption of "no first use" on our part would have any effect on the present Iranian regime. On the other hand, our national leaders do not seem to have any realistic clue as to how we can prevent Iran from developing nuclear weapons.

Mitt Romney, when running for president in 2012, vowed that Iran would not get nuclear weapons if he were in charge. But he proffered no plan for accomplishing this particular goal. And when he was running for president in 2008, I asked him, at a public meeting, whether he would consider adopting a "no first use" policy; his answer indicated he would "make no change" in U. S. policy with respect to nuclear weapons.

Since World War II, U. S. presidents have been shadowed by a man carrying U. S. nuclear weapon "launch codes." President John F. Kennedy had to seriously consider the use of nuclear weapons at the time of the Cuban "Missile Crisis" in 1962. But in general, U. S. presidents in the post-war era appear to have given little thought as to what to do about the possibility of having to actually order the use of our nuclear weapons, and have been content to maintain a "keep 'em guessing" policy with respect to nuclear weapons.

Former Secretary of Defense Robert McNamara wrote extensively about nuclear weapons policy; most memorably, he said that

> . . . nuclear weapons serve no military purpose whatsoever. They are totally useless—except only to deter one's opponent from using them.

Iran continues to deny it is trying to attain a nuclear weapons capability. Israel is known to have had that capability for years, and it is hard to believe that Israel would sit idly by with sworn enemy Iran in possession of nuclear weapons. U. S. policy remains a question mark, especially since the U. S. is the only nation that has actually used nuclear weapons against an enemy, and since the U. S. president, acting alone and as commander in chief, is the ***only*** person who can actually order the use of U. S. nuclear weapons.

To me, the situation seems unstable, and I think that consideration of my proposed No First Use constitutional amendment by Congress would be a beneficial development.

I personally believe that the United Nations will eventually consider a worldwide ban on the use of nuclear and radioactive weapons by one nation state against another. In this connection, I believe it would be wise policy for the U. S. to develop a large, new manned bomber that would be capable of dropping or launching the huge, nonnuclear weapons that it has developed in the years since the end of World War II.

Using stealth technology to make its radar image tiny or non-existent, and laser guidance for its weapons, the huge nonnuclear weapons could create a blast effect the size of Hiroshima, without the residual killing effects of nuclear weapons. Because these weapons are both large and heavy, they are impractical as missile warheads. It is unlikely that other countries would have the resources needed to loft such huge weapons, so the U. S. would have a practical monopoly of them.

The ban on nuclear weapons would thus benefit the U. S. strategic position in the world. Use of nuclear weapons would amount to war crimes. The big nonnuclear weapons could not be banned, as a practical matter, because they would differ from smaller nonnuclear weapons only in degree, and not in quality. The U. S. can use the big nonnuclear weapons now, but only by hauling them around in big transport aircraft; the aircraft I am proposing would be a more practical way of employing these weapons, which in the future would functionally replace nuclear weapons. (Continued *possession of its nuclear weapons* by the U. S., coupled with the No First Use amendment, would help ensure against cheating.)

Once the use of nuclear weapons is banned, no country will develop them. In fact, a country like Iran would have no purpose in developing nuclear weapons, since they could not be employed without making the user a war criminal. This might be the best way of dealing with the Iranian situation. Think about it.

I added the last sentence to my proposal in order to make it clear that our nuclear weapons might eventually be used to defend the planet from space objects such as asteroids, a threat that appeared all too real, as a result of a big asteroid's near miss that occurred in February, 2013. Public attention to that possibility resulted from widespread publication of spectacular photos of a meteor that hurtled through Russian airspace at about the same time, causing widespread structural damage including hundreds of broken windows and actual physical injuries, some of which required hospitalization, to a lot of people.

SECTION THREE

Other Ideas for Consideration

A GRADING SYSTEM FOR THE TWENTY-FIRST CENTURY

The grading system used by most public high schools in the United States comes to us by way of tradition. It has five broad categories: A, B, C, D, and F. You will notice that it has no grade of E; more about that, shortly.

Four of the five categories are for grades that are considered "Passing." The student receives course credit for grades A through D, usually on a four-point scale: A is worth 4.0 points, B is worth 3.0 points, C is worth 2.0 points, and D is assigned a value of 1.0 point.

The fifth category, F, is worthless, 0 points. The student who receives a grade of F for "failure" has nothing to show for the time he or she spent in the class. No course credit is given for a grade of F.

The significant thing is that the student who gets an F makes no progress toward what presumably is the reason he or she is going to school in the first place, which is to "graduate" with a high school diploma, today's admission ticket to consideration for any but the most menial of employment possibilities.

It is no accident that the overwhelming majority of those who wind up in prison in this country share a common characteristic; they did not graduate from high school. They were high school drop-outs. They lacked the ticket needed to get a job. So they turned to crime, and earned a ticket to the slammer.

Huge amounts of tax money are spent annually in this country in a vain attempt to remedy this situation, to improve drop-out rates, graduation rates, and so on. Earlier in this decade, the U. S. Department of Education announced five important "performance goals" for the public educational system: fifth on the list was really the most important: "All students will graduate from high school." (This was in the Elementary and Secondary Education Act, or ESEA, as amended by the No Child Left Behind Act, or NCLB, which is up for renewal from time to time.) And as every "stakeholder" in the field of public education well knows, the U. S. isn't anywhere *near* that most important performance goal, the one that says: "All students will graduate from high school."

Quite frankly, the U. S. Department of Education can flog the state education departments with every kind of testing requirement, every type of statistical hoop that the DOE's bureaucrats can dream up, and the students will *still* drop out (at an average rate of 7,000 students per *day*, according to one yardstick) and fail to graduate (and many will wind up in jail), . . . *until*: and now, I'm going to show you how to solve the problem.

Who am I, to make bold with a solution? I'm a teacher, with more than 20 years of experience, teaching in the public schools. And I'm a lawyer (who has also run for political office), with more than 50 years of legal and public affairs experience. In 1990, I wrote a paper for a class that I was taking, in which I described the modification to the traditional grading system that I propose here, in an effort to help solve the thorny problems that continue to vex and puzzle the educational establishment.

Here's the solution: *stop* giving the grade of F, except to signify "Failure to attend class." *Start* giving the grade of E, which signifies "Exposure to subject matter." And for the grade of E, which is a *passing* grade meaning that the student receives credit for the course, assign the point value of 0.5.

Graduation rates will soar and dropout rates will plunge if schools will make this one, simple change in the traditional grading system!

What I have done here is propose a "no fail" grading system. Stop labeling, as failures, those students who regularly attend classes and who honestly try to learn, but who simply happen to wind up at the bottom of the heap, grade-wise.

As an experienced teacher, I can tell you that any student in a class where I am the teacher will learn *something*. And he or she will deserve the appropriate grade/credit for that learning. To label that student a *failure* just because he or she is at the bottom is ridiculous!

I know very well that some teachers will object to this change. Some teachers seem to believe that giving a student a grade of F is a way of punishing the student (which teachers who can't any longer spank students, whose behavior is often out of line, will be reluctant to give up). And some teachers will substitute expulsion from class, which will result in an F, for failure to attend class.

Nothing is perfect. Certainly, it will behoove lazy students to just "sit there" in a non-disruptive manner and fail to perform, just to be able to get credit for a class that they don't find interesting. Or whatever.

And I do not mean to suggest that it would be O. K. for a lot of students to try to graduate with an "E" average. It is up to the schools to require a meaningful level of learning (performance). There are several other reforms that should be considered; here are a few of them:

1. Allow students to repeat any class (perhaps up to five times, without permission to repeat more than five times). Allow students to substitute a higher, later grade for an earlier, lower grade.

2. Require students to stay awake, alert, and non-disruptive in class, giving each student a maximum number of unexcused absences per term, with the teacher to have discretion as to whether or not the student's behavior for a particular day warrants counting the student present.

3. Allow the teacher discretion (within limits) as to a minimum level of performance; for example, to get a grade for the day, the student must turn in the assignment for the day, substantially done; otherwise, the student is effectively counted absent for the day.

[Obviously, the student has to show up. And the student must attempt to do the assignments. The grade modification suggested here is that the student gets credit for showing up and doing the assignments as well as he or she can; the student is given credit for what he or she does and is not labeled a failure simply for being at the bottom of the class.]

4. This is very important. By eliminating the fear of failing, the school is now able to encourage, or even require, students to take classes that they would otherwise not take. For example, a school could require that every student take Calculus!

Ever since I saw the movie, "Stand and Deliver," I have thought about requiring that every student take Calculus. "Stand and Deliver" was filmed with actors playing the part of students, but the story was true, proving to me that, properly taught, using "cookbook" step-by-step methods, it is possible for all students to learn Calculus, just like it is possible for all students to learn to read and write.

I'm using Calculus here to symbolize the fact that, in the Twenty-First Century, our high school graduates need to develop more math skills than has been the case in the past. It is possible for even the smallest, poorest schools to teach Calculus, because all you need is a good teacher and a good textbook; you don't need fancy lab equipment to be able to teach Calculus.

(If you saw "Stand and Deliver," you may recall that the new teacher was supposed to teach about computers but the inner-city LA school didn't get the computers, so he turned to teaching Calculus instead, and the other teachers all hooted at him, insisting their students were not capable of learning Calculus: *did he ever prove them wrong!)*

A lot of students will whine about their lack of ability to pass Calculus; let them whine, because schools can guarantee that, if they show up and make an honest effort, they cannot fail Calculus! The no-fail grading system allows every student the opportunity to take a "hard" course like Calculus is supposed to be, and inevitably, some students who normally would avoid taking Calculus will find that they actually like it and can do well in it!

Thus it is that the no-fail grading system, proposed here, has many potential benefits beyond simply improving graduation rates and ameliorating the dropout statistics. "No-fail" is fairer than the traditional grading system, and it is, indeed, A Grading System for the Twenty-First Century!

Apart from the benefits of the "no fail" grading system set forth above, there is a significant additional benefit of the "no fail" grading system that has nothing directly to do with improving high school graduation rates.

Students who participate in high school athletics, as well as those who participate in other extracurricular activities such as band, chorus, drama, orchestra, and the like, often have their participation interrupted by a huge shock in the form of a failing grade in a course they neglected, perforce.

It wasn't that they deliberately neglected that course in which they received an F. It was simply the fact that there are only 24 hours in everyone's day, even the day of a talented young performer, caught up in the whirl of striving for perfection.

The rules may say that, talented or not, school must come first, and one failing grade may sideline such a performer for a time, despite the needs of the team. Thus, the student athlete may be required to "sit out" as much as a whole season, as a penalty for striving, or so it seems.

Fair or not, rules are rules, and woe is often to the student athlete, who may be a team star, and whose absence at a critical time may cost his team a championship and himself, a scholarship or other benefit.

It hardly seems fair, and the suffering may spread far beyond the person directly affected—to his coach, his team, his class, and his school.

Here's where the proposed "no fail" grading system may make a difference. The sure way of eliminating the nasty, red "F" is the installation of a *passing* grade of "E" as a substitute. While it is possible that the "powers that be" will simply attempt to attach equal vilification to the substitute, it will undoubtedly be difficult, politically, for them to do so. It is, after all, time to end such crude penalties for those who strive to excel, whether in sports or in other extracurricular activities.

In any event, an attempt to reinstitute the sanction of forced idleness against a talented young performer may well fail—as it should. Today's emphasis favors participation in extracurricular activities of all kinds as a worthy extension of scholarly pursuits, and such participation should not be withheld merely because of a low grade.

The traditional grading system is strongly entrenched. Efforts to replace A, B, C, and D with some other system, usually numerical, have largely failed. The A, B, C, and D marks are easy to understand, and in this country, at least, are so universal as to be sacrosanct.

Not so, the grade of F. While easily translated as "failure," the grade of F is an anomaly. It does not follow the A, B, C, D sequence. In fact, the next letter in the sequence, the letter E, is missing from the traditional grading system.

Obviously, the grade of E that I suggested as a substitute for the grade of F fits perfectly into the traditional grading system. What also fits in is the notion that the grade of E, like the others—A, B, C, and D—is, like them, a *passing* grade. It is, to be sure, the lowest passing grade, as A is the highest, but there is nothing wrong with the idea that E, like the others, is a passing grade and is, therefore, entitled to the respect given the others in the A, B, C, D sequence.

In other words, there is nothing about the grade of E to suggest that it should not be respected as a passing grade. I previously suggested that the E could stand for "Exposure to subject matter," and I was not being facetious in making such a suggestion. On the contrary, I was simply being practical; the grade of C, meaning "Average," is shunned by those seeking admission to the higher realms of academia, and the grade of D has an implication that is only too obvious.

No top student will want a grade of E to grace his or her scholastic efforts, and no institution of higher learning worthy of the name will give very serious consideration to a student whose transcript is peppered with such grades. On the other hand, an "E" here and there probably will not disqualify a star athlete, the admission of whom is important to the school's sports program.

There is another reason for modifying the traditional grading system in the way that I suggest. Consider the situation of the extra-curricular participant. At the present time, he or she faces a dilemma of excruciating proportions. As a top student, he or she intends to pursue admission to, say, medical school. Certain very demanding courses are needed as prerequisites for admission. But the student faces a high risk of failure in taking such courses while at the same time attempting to participate at a high level in the extracurricular activity, whether as an athlete or perhaps as a star musical performer. At the present time, the only way out appears to be opting out—of either the needed but demanding course, or of the extracurricular activity itself. The risk of failure is simply too great.

To the rescue comes the grade of E. While the top student obviously does not want the grade of E on his transcript, he or she can avoid the almost catastrophic risk of a failing grade, and the setback to his academic progress that a grade of F will certainly cause. A grade of E furnishes the student with a tolerable risk because it will not cause him or her to be ejected from the activity, and it will not cause loss of progress toward graduation. Saved from the stress of the high risk dilemma, the student can go forward with the needed course work without having to abandon the extracurricular activity.

The advantages to all parties concerned of the no-fail grading system that I have suggested are so manifest that the adoption of the system by virtually any U. S. school district should be a no-brainer. The cost is essentially zero, the advantages are huge, and there is absolutely no offense to the traditional grading system, as I have demonstrated above.

But how to get it done? First of all, it is more than apparent that adoption of the no-fail grading system I have described is beyond the ability of any individual teacher. On the other hand, teachers as a group, properly organized and motivated, should be able to persuade even the most reluctant school board that the no-fail system is the way to go, perhaps beginning with the next term, or perhaps even sooner.

Who else could persuade a school board? Well, how about a group of parents, perhaps organized through a parent-teacher organization? Or, how about a group of sports enthusiasts? How about the school district's athletic coaches? They might have considerable influence.

Could the local newspaper, or the local radio station, somehow be of some assistance? And how about the taxpayers in general, and as individuals. Perhaps you yourself could help focus attention on the need for a change in the traditional grading system. For example, try giving each member of the board a copy of this article. Or, write a letter to the editor of the newspaper. Or, collect signatures on a petition.

The superintendent of schools in your district might be interested in the modification of the traditional grading system that I have suggested, but don't pin your hopes on the superintendent. He or she probably has enough high priority issues to deal with, and while he or she might be sympathetic with the idea of altering the traditional grading system, there is only the tiniest possibility that the superintendent is going to be willing to put his or her job on the line in order to get the school board to give this proposal the nod.

Public school people tend to be very conservative. The innovative educator is actually a rarity; pardon me for relating this little anecdote, but it will illustrate the problem. I "invented" this idea for a no-fail modification of the traditional grading system while taking a graduate education course back in 1990. I wrote it up then, and presented it to my class of perhaps 20 or so other graduate students in education, and I had the distinct impression that the other students were favorably impressed. So what happened? Nothing, so far as I can tell. They pursued their professional careers, presumably in the field of education, and presumably with knowledge of what they could do to improve the high school drop-out problem. You would think that some of them, at least, would do something about the problem, and that it would be solved by now.

But you would be wrong. In fact, if anything, the high school dropout problem has continued to worsen, because the grading systems in use now are essentially unchanged since 1990, and the prison population continues to have the same characteristic I mentioned at the beginning of this article; the inmates, generally speaking, did not graduate from high school, and lacking the ticket of admission to most jobs, they tended to wind up in the slammer.

The professional educators, for the most part, continue clueless. You who read this article can help them, and I hope you will. You will have to be insistently persistant—and I hope you will. But let not another generation pass, and suffer, with the shortcomings of the traditional grading system. Try the modification I suggested here, and then be patient; it probably will take several years before the changes in graduation statistics manifest themselves, but change they will, and as a result, we will inch toward the goal, the one that says, "All students will graduate from high school." It will be harder to measure the benefits of the "no fail" system to those who participate in extracurricular activities, but you can be confident that the efforts of people like yourself will be felt in the years ahead, as you help implement A Grading System for the Twenty-First Century.

AIRPORTS FOR THE TWENTY-FIRST CENTURY

It was July 17, 2007, a rainy day in Sao Paulo, Brazil's largest city. The TAM airlines Airbus A320 flight had originated in Porto Alegre and now was landing on Sao Paulo's Congonhas Airport main runway; the big jet was hurtling toward the end of the 6,362-foot concrete ribbon. The smiles on the faces of friends and relatives waiting to greet the 175 passengers aboard were now being replaced by looks of horror.

Moments from the certain impact awaiting the orange-tailed jetliner as it ran out of runway, the pilot desperately yanked back on the control yoke and opened the throttles, causing the heavily-loaded aircraft to soar over a crowded roadway, then smash into a large fuel station and an office building.

Within moments, all aboard the jet and several persons on the ground were incinerated by flames that reached 1,800 degrees F.; the total death toll was expected to near 200, making this Brazil's greatest aircraft disaster.

The president of Brazil responded by promising Sao Paulo a new airport, presumably, one with longer runways. Meanwhile, leading aircraft manufacturers promised bigger planes that will put even more pressure on the world's airports, which were planned and built during the 20th century. Few existing airports have runways that are even close to adequate for today's jetliners, and as a practical matter, the airports that will be able to accommodate the giant airliners of tomorrow have yet to be built.

For example, it was only a short time ago that the gigantic Airbus A380 was unveiled, a double-deck jetliner that will be able to seat more than 800 passengers. With a wingspan of nearly 265 feet, the world's largest passenger jet will be able to carry more than one million pounds of gross weight into the air. That's if the new giant jet can find any place to land with all that bulk.

Now that the twenty-first century, the second airline century, is underway, it is high time to look ahead and begin to view the future of airline travel.

That future must include new jetport facilities with much longer runways. Think runways that are about ten miles long!

There are two crucial points in the flight of every jetliner--when the jet is taking off, and again when it is landing. What I am proposing is that every major airport have two parallel runways, one for takeoffs and the other for landings. Both such runways should be about 50,000 feet long, approximately ten miles long.

I propose that aircraft which are taking off be positioned at the very end of the runway. Each jet would head down the runway, gathering speed and developing lift. When the plane is ready to lift off the runway, it would keep going, straight down the runway, developing more and more altitude as the runway drops off below. If something bad happens within those first moments of flight, the pilot may be able to simply ease the plane back down onto the runway, and let it roll comfortably to a stop.

Many fatal airline accidents have occurred during takeoff (recall that the Brazilian jetliner accident with which I opened this article was, in one sense, an accident on takeoff, even though that plane had actually landed, was running out of runway, and tried to take off again). There are all sorts of accidents that have taken place during the takeoff phase, caused by such things as birds (being ingested in the jet engines, causing the engines to lose power); mechanical failure (again causing loss of engine power); fires (in the engine, causing loss of power); and similar events. In many cases, the planes involved have tried to continue the takeoff, have become airborne, and too often have crashed (and also burned, due to the fact that the plane is usually fully loaded with volatile fuel). Many pilots and their aircrews and passengers would be alive today if they had available nearly ten miles of runway stretching out in front of them that might have permitted them to ease a floundering aircraft back down onto the runway again.

This latter type of accident illustrates the folly of trying to economize by making the runways somewhat less than ten miles in length; if anything, ten miles should be viewed as the minimum safe length, and runways of more than ten miles should be considered.

So far, I have been talking about the takeoff runways; now, I want to discuss the ten-mile-long landing runways. To illustrate my point, let me cite the case of the Aeroflot Tupolev 134A that was trying to land at Ivanovo, Russia, on August 27, 1992. The jetliner was coming in on an approach that was both fast and steep when it crashed about two miles short of the runway, killing all 84 persons aboard.

Under my proposal, the normal glide path to the ten mile long landing runway would have the jetliner touching down at about the 25,000-foot mark, i.e., about half-way down the ten mile long landing runway. However, the point of touchdown would be at the pilot's discretion, and thus, if the pilot felt the need to land the plane two miles short of the usual touchdown point, it would not be a problem; the runway would be there, and the pilot would be able to land the plane safely (this assumes, of course, that the pilot has the plane properly configured for landing and with the proper airspeed for a safe landing).

From the point of normal touchdown, the plane would have more than 25,000 feet of runway ahead, which should be more than enough rollout space for even the biggest, heaviest planes. Even if the pilot touched down a couple of miles farther down the runway than usual, the plane would still have about 15,000 feet of runway ahead of it.

Think of it this way: if the pilot of the Brazilian jet had 15,000 feet of runway to work with instead of 6,362, he and nearly 200 other people would still be alive.

Landing on a ten mile long runway the way I am proposing means that the plane is over runway for five miles before the point of normal touchdown. The pilot can bring the plane on down at any time during that five miles, and the plane will NOT crash short of the runway, as so often happens, with fatal results.

There are all kinds of possible reasons for the pilot to suddenly wish to bring the plane on down, such as wind shear or other weather-related events, engine failure, fuel exhaustion, etc. The pilot has the option of landing earlier than planned or earlier than usual, something the pilot normally lacks with today's airports.

By this point, I may have convinced you that ten mile runways are a good idea, but implementing my proposal may be deemed impractical. Where would we be able to locate such a huge airport, as a practical matter?

My answer is: locate the ten mile runways out of the city, where the land is both available and relatively cheap. For the sake of discussion, let's assume that relatively level land is available, out a ways. We probably need a strip of land that is somewhere between ½ a mile to a mile in width, and at least ten miles long, with control against man-made obstructions such as tall buildings or broadcast towers extending much farther out. So we are talking about five to ten square miles of land, some of which probably can be cultivated.

But I'm mindful of the fact that millions of dollars may have been invested in the existing airport facilities, closer in. I suggest continued use of such facilities, in most cases. Small aircraft can continue to use the "old" airport facilities. Existing parking lots, terminal buildings, and associated facilities (such as hotels and motels) can continue to be used.

Existing security facilities also can be used. All we have to do is arrange for passengers (and air crew members) to be transported quickly and efficiently to and from the new airport runway facilities (and of course, aircraft storage and maintenance facilities).

The answer: shuttle transportation. The method? Helicopters. But more likely, dedicated rail, either conventional rail or, my favorite, monorail. (Bus transport via dedicated roadway might be a relatively cheap alternative.) The neat thing about monorail, (and here I'm talking about something similar to the monorail used at Florida's Disney World to transport customers between the far-flung parking lots and the Magic Kingdom), lies in the fact that the monorail route can use minimal land area and can use the air above existing roadways and small buildings.

In some cases, it may be most economical to use something like dedicated buses to begin with, to keep costs down, replacing the buses eventually with, perhaps, a monorail setup. (It should be noted that such buses, equipped with internal combustion engines, could burn non-polluting hydrogen, made from water by electrolysis, with the electric power coming from wind-powered generators).

While I am discussing the siting of ten mile runways in distant rural areas, I should mention a couple of other points:

There is no need for every old airport to be replicated with ten mile runways. It makes no sense, for example, for both Washington, D. C., and Baltimore, Md. to build ten mile runways; they could join forces to build one set of ten mile runways that could serve both of these nearby cities. Another example: Los Angeles International is not that far from the Burbank Airport, and there may very well be land near the latter that would be suitable for a set of ten mile runways.

Also, Rome was not built in a day, and even if ten-mile runways are a good idea (as they are), it's going to take some cooperation, and some real vision, to make them a reality. Also, some time. It may very well be the case that some cities are just not going to get service from the very biggest new jets, such as the Airbus A380, anytime soon. So be it. The big planes are a near-term reality, but it may take some disasters to prod airport planners in the direction of doing the right thing.

Such a disaster came very close to happening one chilly day, early in 2009. The saga of Flight 1549 began, innocently enough, on a Thursday, about mid-afternoon. U. S. Airways Captain Chesley B. Sullenberger III, a veteran pilot who started his flying career with U. S. Air Force fighter jets, was in command when Flight 1549 began its takeoff roll down one of LaGuardia Airport's two 7,000-foot runways.

It was a little past 2:25 p.m., New York time when Flight 1549 made contact with the Terminal Radar Approach Facility (TRACON). Only seconds later, Flight 1549 told TRACON that they had "hit birds." Continuing, the flight reported: "We lost thrust in both engines, we're turning back towards LaGuardia." I am quoting, now, from the official transcript, released Feb. 2, 2009 by the FAA (Federal Aviation Administration). The time of this transmission was 2:27:36 p.m.

Captain Sullenberger (Sully, to those who knew him well) had taken the controls of the big Airbus A320 (the same type of aircraft that had been involved in the tragic Brazilian accident with which I opened this article.) First Officer Jeffrey B. Skiles was trying to restart the engines. The possibility of returning to LaGuardia was quickly abandoned; there were simply too many buildings and too many people who would be at risk. The realization that their Airbus A320 had just become a big glider when a flock of birds, apparently Canadian geese, was encountered, caused both pilots to realize that they, the three flight attendants, and the 150 passengers aboard Flight 1549, were suddenly in danger of crashing down into New York City; the potential death toll was horrific.

Only seconds after rejecting the option of trying to return to LaGuardia, another possibility was considered. Just over a minute later, Flight 1549 asked: "What's over to our right, anything in New Jersey, maybe Teterboro?"

TRACON responded: "O. K., off to your right side is Teterboro Airport. Do you want to try and go to Teterboro?" Answer: "Yes."

Teterboro Airport in Bergen County, New Jersey is ten miles distant from LaGuardia. A 7,000-foot runway, oriented north-south, was available; a hospital was less than two miles distant.

TRACON contacted Teterboro immediately and cleared Flight 1549 for landing on its main runway. At 2:29:21 TRACON told 1549: "You can land runway one at Teterboro." The instantaneous response was: "We can't do it."

Teterboro Airport has another, somewhat shorter runway, so TRACON said: "O.K., which runway would you like at Teterboro?"

More than a minute earlier, Flight 1549 had warned that "We may end up in the Hudson." Now, at 2:29:28, Flight 1549 made it official. "We're gonna be in the Hudson."

As an experienced glider pilot, Captain Sullenberger knew that the A320, without thrust from either of its big engines, could not make it even as far as Teterboro Airport, which he could clearly see, off to his right, as he turned south along the Hudson River. The main obstacle ahead was the George Washington bridge.

What happened next happened very fast. Flight 1549 soared over the George Washington bridge, the towers of which extend about 600 feet into the air, the suspension cables sagging much lower. The big plane disappeared from radar screens. In a "Sixty Minutes" broadcast aired Feb. 9, 2009 on CBS, Captain Sullenberger described the task he had faced to Katie Couric and a nationwide audience: "I needed to touch down with the wings exactly level. I needed to touch down with the nose slightly up. I needed to touch down at a descent rate that was survivable. And I needed to touch down just above our minimum flying speed, but not below it. And I needed to make all these things happen simultaneously."

The fact that he did all of these things, perfectly, was evident to millions of people who watched on television that chilly January 15th afternoon as rescue vessels converged on the aircraft, floating in the Hudson River. Many passengers, after quickly exiting the downed plane, stood on the wings, waiting to be picked up. From a distance, they appeared to be walking on the water. For many, the feeling was that they were walking on air.

All 155 persons aboard Flight 1549 survived what could only be described as an ordeal. They had departed LaGuardia on what was supposed to be a routine flight to Charlotte, North Carolina, about 400 miles distant. And of course, they never got there, that day at least.

Some days afterward, they met together at Charlotte, where Captain Sullenberger and the other four members of his crew received applause and hugs from the grateful survivors of Flight 1549. The skills of pilots Sullenberger and Skiles, as well as the flight attendants who got the passengers out of the aircraft quickly and efficiently, were frequently remarked upon.

In the days that followed, the plane was hoisted up out of the water by a big crane. An engine that had broken loose was located by divers on the bottom of the river; it, too, was recovered and subjected to close scrutiny. There was no doubt, at all, about the cause of this forced ditching; big birds had, indeed, been ingested by both engines, causing both to cease operating.

A freak accident? Not at all; bird strikes are a common aircraft hazard, and the loss of power in one jet engine due to bird ingestion is the reason why many flights are aborted, every year. What is rare is complete loss of power in more than one engine, leading to a crash of some kind in an aircraft that has only two engines, such as the Airbus A320.

When I wrote this article in 2008, in which I proposed that every major airport should have two parallel runways "about 50,000 feet long, approximately ten miles long," I did not expect to have an event that would so dramatically endorse my proposal, so publicly and so soon. The very first thing I mentioned as providing a rationale for my proposal was "birds (being ingested in the jet engines, causing the engines to lose power)." But, there it is, and there I am, vindicated.

In the first edition of my book MELTDOWN! I wrote that "it may take some disasters to prod airport planners in the direction of doing the right thing, in order to bring about Airports for the Twenty-First Century."

Fortunately, those aboard Flight 1549 had a highly skilled pilot in Captain Sullenberger, who also was an experienced glider pilot, for that is what the U.S. Air A320 became, a big glider, when the birds ingested by both engines brought both to full stop within a matter of seconds. The glider pilot instincts of Captain Sullenberger were what enabled him to save the day; the lives of 155 persons, including his own, were at risk, and a pilot lacking those glider pilot instincts might not have been equal to the task with which he suddenly, and without warning, was confronted. Being a glider pilot might have only been a hobby, with him, but they gave him the winning margin.

I have no intention of asking Captain Sullenberger whether he thought he might have been able to get back down onto the runway if he had started with a runway ten miles long, as I proposed. The point is that he did not have that option; without doubt, he would have flown Flight 1549 differently, if he had ten miles of runway in front of him, when he started his takeoff roll. The runways at LaGuardia each are about 7,000 feet long; the easy thing to do is scoff with "where are we going to get another 43,000 feet of runway?" and forget the whole idea as impossible.

Obviously, I can't produce another 43,000 feet of runway out of my hat, and neither can anyone else. LaGuardia Airport opened for business in 1939, more than 70 years ago. For that matter, Teterboro goes back another 20 years, making it the oldest major airport in the New York Metropolitan Area. These old airports are products of the early days of aviation, of the first airline century. Neither of them are even close to being capable of handling the A380 giants which are now going into service, worldwide.

Let's get real; airports like LaGuardia and Teterboro are obsolete. Airports like New York's Kennedy are able to handle the A380, but the truth is that even Kennedy is stretched to the limit by such a giant aircraft. And we are, now, little more than a tenth of the way into the Twenty-First Century.

What lies ahead? Giant supersonic transports? Aircraft that soar into orbit, in near space? How about aircraft which regularly dock at the International Space Station? At what point are we going to be looking at lunar travelers? At flights to Mars? Do you think I am being fanciful?

There isn't a single one of these possibilities that can be totally ruled out for the time remaining in the Twenty-First Century. And there isn't a single one of these possibilities that can comfortably be accommodated by the commercial airport facilities existing now or even on the drawing boards for the future. Take a look at the ideas that H. G. Wells wrote about. His contemporaries may have scoffed at him a good deal. But do we?

Scoff not. Take a look, instead, at my ideas for ten mile runways. To be sure, they are far out--literally. To be sure, the idea of even talking about where to put them seems almost absurd. Just remember this: the people who told Wilbur and Orville that "it'll never fly" are all dead and forgotten. We honor the Wright Brothers. What they did at Kitty Hawk happened more than 100 years ago. Consider the next 100.

By the way, Captain Sullenberger is retired now, four years after his dramatic landing in the Hudson. According to *Politico*, he is at the University of California, Berkley, as a visiting scholar with the Center for Catastrophic Risk Management.

A WOMAN'S RIGHT TO CHOOSE

A woman living in the United States who has children will, on average, have two children. That's according to the U. S. Census Bureau. A woman living in the United States, in normal health, will have about 300 opportunities to have children over her reproductive lifetime of about 25 years. That's simple math: 12 opportunities per year (about once a month), times 25 years, equals 300 total opportunities to have children, as shown on the accompanying chart.

Women do not have children by themselves; they require input from a male partner. However, women in the United States have a legal right to choose their male partners; no male, not even a husband, has the legal right to require any particular woman, not even a wife, to allow him to input her at any particular time. In short, the woman has a right to choose her male sexual partner and to choose the occasions that her male partner inputs her.

What if a woman receives input from a male that she does not want to receive? We call this rape.

If the rape results in her becoming pregnant, we allow her to seek medical assistance in terminating her unwanted pregnancy.

Or, what if a woman receives input from a close male relative, without regard to whether she is willing or not; we call this incest, and again, we allow her to obtain medical assistance to terminate the pregnancy.

Finally, the more difficult case, where a woman willingly receives input from a male partner, becomes pregnant (perhaps accidentally), and then decides she wants to terminate the pregnancy. **A normal, healthy woman in the United States can expect to have about 300 opportunities to have a child during her reproductive lifetime (12 per year, for 25 years). According to the U. S. Census Bureau, a woman in the U. S. who has children will, on average, have two children (in other words, she will use two of those 300 opportunities to have a child). The question is, who will choose *which two* of the opportunities she will use: the woman herself, or someone else? *Someone* must make that choice, in every case.** **(See chart on the next page.)**

Chart Showing Lifetime Reproductive Possibilities for U. S.Women

Yr 1	1	2	3	4	5	6	7	8	9	10	11	12
Yr 2	13	14	15	16	17	18	19	20	21	22	23	24
Yr 3	25	26	27	28	29	30	31	32	33	34	35	36
Yr 4	37	38	39	40	41	42	43	44	45	46	47	48
Yr 5	49	50	51	52	53	54	55	56	57	58	59	60
Yr 6	61	62	63	64	65	66	67	68	69	70	71	72
Yr 7	73	74	75	76	77	78	79	80	81	82	83	84
Yr 8	85	86	87	88	89	90	91	92	93	94	95	96
Yr 9	97	98	99	100	101	102	103	104	105	106	107	108
Yr 10	109	110	111	112	113	114	115	116	117	118	119	120
Yr 11	121	122	123	124	125	126	127	128	129	130	131	132
Yr 12	133	134	135	136	137	138	139	140	141	142	143	144
Yr 13	145	146	147	148	149	150	151	152	153	154	155	156
Yr 14	157	158	159	160	161	162	163	164	165	166	167	168
Yr 15	169	170	171	172	173	174	175	176	177	178	179	180
Yr 16	181	182	183	184	185	186	187	188	189	190	191	192
Yr 17	193	194	195	196	197	198	199	200	201	202	203	204
Yr 18	205	206	207	208	209	210	211	212	213	214	215	216
Yr 19	217	218	219	220	221	222	223	224	225	226	227	228
Yr 20	229	230	231	232	233	234	235	236	237	238	239	240
Yr 21	241	242	243	244	245	246	247	248	249	250	251	252
Yr 22	253	254	255	256	257	258	259	260	261	262	263	264
Yr 23	265	266	267	268	269	270	271	272	273	274	275	276
Yr 24	277	278	279	280	281	282	283	284	285	286	287	288
Yr 25	289	290	291	292	293	294	295	296	297	298	299	300

For about four decades, women in the United States, in reliance on the U. S. Supreme Court decision in *Roe v. Wade*, have had the legal right to terminate a pregnancy under these latter circumstances. However, many women now fear that this right may soon be gone, in light of the more recent 5-4 Supreme Court decision in the case of *Gonzales v. Carhart,* which some will view as reflective of changes that have taken place in the makeup of the Court.

American society has been split over this issue far too long.

One large group opposes allowing a woman to change her mind. Members of this group say they are pro-life. They exalt the pregnancy and claim to protect the rights of what they see as the unborn child. They insist that a pregnancy, once begun, must be protected, and extreme proponents of this viewpoint would not allow termination of a pregnancy under any circumstances, even if it is the result of rape or incest. They equate abortion to murder.

The other large group exalts the rights of the woman to choose to terminate any pregnancy, for any reason, at any time. Members of this group proclaim that they are pro-choice.

Who is right? Which viewpoint should prevail? Is an unborn child entitled to any protection, at any time, prior to birth? Up to this time, the terms of the debate have been as summarized above. What I am suggesting is that a new look needs to be taken at this controversy.

The new perspective should begin with the facts I stated at the outset. If we assume that the average adult woman in the U. S. has about 300 opportunities to have a child, during her reproductive lifetime, and that women who have children will each have, on average, two children, then the question becomes simply this:

Who has the right to determine which two, of 300 opportunities, a particular woman will utilize? The possible choices are:

1. The woman herself.

2. The woman's male partner.

3. The larger society (i.e., the government).

Make no mistake. If you are "pro-life," you are saying that someone *other than the woman herself* has the right to make this decision, that is, to choose which two, of 300 opportunities, a particular woman must utilize to have her children. In general, you are asserting that either the larger society (the government) must decide, or else you are suggesting that the woman's male partner (such as her husband) has the right to make this decision for her.

If you are "pro-choice," then you are saying that the woman herself has the right to control her own reproductive destiny, to have essentially complete control over her own body. She decides, by herself, which two of 300 opportunities she will utilize to have her children.

Most people, who are pro-life, are simply repeating a litany: abortion is murder. They do not realize what they are doing, *i.e.,* asserting *that only the government* has the right to control the body of a particular woman. Most pro-life people would *instantly* reject the pro-life position, if they were aware of its implications.

The pro-choice position, where the woman controls her own body, free from government interference, is the only position that is consistent with notions of individual liberty and the constitutional rights that most Americans enjoy.

But what about the unborn child? What rights, if any, does the unborn child have, consistent with the pro-choice position?

The only reasonable, sensible position to take is that the unborn child begins to acquire rights of his/her own at the point where the child could live an independent life outside the mother's womb, whether or not the child is actually born at that point, or at some later point. This is the point of viability. It does not imply viability only by heroic medical means. It means, instead, normal or reasonable viability, and is a fairly bright-line concept, at approximately six months after conception.

At that point, it is reasonable for society as a whole (i.e. the government, on behalf of "all of us,") to assume the role of protector of the unborn child from any interference except for measures medically necessary to preserve the mother's life, which should be paramount for the balance of the pregnancy, that is, until the point that the child is actually born.

During the final three months of pregnancy, the woman no longer has a right to choose; her right to choose is exercisable during only the first six months of pregnancy. After that, choice is no longer an option but measures needed to preserve the mother's life continue to be superior to any rights of the unborn child, until the child emerges from the womb.

At birth, the child is a new, separate individual, with the rights of an individual, subject to the societal interest in raising the child to maturity (adulthood) through care and education, which is a responsibility shared by the parents of the child and society as a whole (government).

An important feature of the pro-choice point of view is the principle of substitution; if a particular pregnancy is aborted, the woman can then substitute a later pregnancy. Thus, since on average she will have two children, her choice is either to continue the pregnancy or to postpone having a child, simply taking advantage of a later opportunity to have a child, substituting the later one for the present one. (If the particular woman already has the children she chooses to have, she has the right to choose not to have another child.)

Since the woman who has children will, on average, have two children, there is no overall diminution in the number of children born. The child actually born is not the same one as the child that would have been born of the earlier pregnancy had that pregnancy not been terminated, but on the other hand, the child born later probably would not have been born at all if the earlier pregnancy had not been terminated. The substituted child is presumably just as worthy and valuable as the child who would have been born earlier, had that pregnancy not been terminated.

From a societal point of view, the woman who has the later child probably will be better prepared, better educated, and better off economically than she would have been earlier. Thus, the exercise of the woman's choice may allow her to produce a "better" child.

The idea that society must restrict abortions in order to save the lives of the "unborn" children is nonsense, when viewed with the principle of substitution in mind; the unborn earlier child is replaced by the later born child. This is one of the main fallacies implicit in the idea of restricting abortion.

The right of a woman to choose, for herself, which of 300 opportunities she will utilize to have a child should be considered a fundamental, legal right and should not be dependent on any Supreme Court decision.

Viewed in this light, there should be no legal restriction on the availability of abortion procedures during the first six months of a pregnancy. Abortions during the final three months of a pregnancy should be available only to save the woman's life and thus are in the nature of medical emergencies. The woman's right to choose an abortion should be subject to the rights of the unborn child during the final three months of pregnancy, since the child is then viable, able to live outside the womb, and should be allowed to do so. In the final trimester, the choice should be to deliver the child, not abort the child.

A minor should have the same right to choose as an adult, since the principle of substitution would be equally applicable. Raising a child is an adult responsibility, and a minor child should not be compelled to take on such an adult responsibility. The parents of a minor girl-child owe her their protection, not their compulsion to take on the adult responsibilities involved in bearing a child while still a minor. Thus, the parents of a minor child who becomes pregnant should support her in a decision to abort a pregnancy that occurs while she is still a minor. She can substitute a later pregnancy--when she is ready to assume the adult role of mother.

Responsible parenthood does not result from the accidental pregnancy that most often motivates women to seek an abortion. It is too important to be undertaken in such a manner. Those who trumpet that they are pro-life and opposed to abortion under any circumstances should realize that what they are advocating will not bring about good results for the children they are claiming to save from abortion. Responsible parenthood is parenthood that results from planned pregnancies, not mere accidents. Responsible parenthood, the parenthood of choice, is the only kind of parenthood that will result in children who have a decent chance to live decent lives.

NOTE: As a practical matter, the pregnancies that most women choose to abort occur as the result of accidents of various kinds, such as failure of a birth control device, or forgetting to take a contraceptive pill, or the unavailability of a condom when needed. And of course, a pregnancy that results from illegal compulsion, such as rape or incest, is obviously a pregnancy that no woman should be required to continue. Also, there are various groups, such as religious organizations, that may try to *influence* a woman's choice, but that cannot actually *require* a particular choice. All pregnancies that a woman chooses to terminate should be terminated as early as practicable; that's obvious. More than 90 per cent of abortions in the U.S. do take place during the first trimester of pregnancy.

THE TRUTH ABOUT ENERGY INDEPENDENCE

In the first edition of this book, I included an article titled "Hurrying Hydrogen." The article ran about 15 pages and was accompanied by its own Bibliography. Most of the article was written in the 2007-2008 period. In this revised and expanded second edition of **MELTDOWN!**, I am including this broader view of the situation in which we find ourselves, in the wake of the 2012 election.

In September of 2012, a few weeks before the election, I wrote an op ed piece that I submitted to the Des Moines *Register*. As far as I know, it was not published at that time, so I will begin with it here, slightly edited but substantially the same as what I wrote at that time:

When a candidate for President of the United States makes a proposal that he cannot possibly deliver on, I think it needs to be pointed out. Mitt Romney made such a proposal in his acceptance speech at the RNC on August 30, 2012.

Toward the end of his speech, Romney announced his, and Paul Ryan's, five steps to their plan to create 12 million new jobs. He said: "First, by 2020, North America will be energy independent . . ." This was not a slip of the tongue. He said NORTH AMERICA. He obviously *meant* to say "North America" because this was in the transcript of his prepared speech, released in advance, which was on the NPR web site, and in the transcript of the speech as he gave it, which was on the Fox News web site—and I myself heard him say it.

Mitt Romney is running for President *of the United States.* He is not running for President of North America, so why would he say this? Canada is obviously not part of the United States.

And assuming he meant to say that the United States will be energy independent by the year 2020 if we elect him, he then proposed to do something that he cannot possibly do. We are already "energy independent" in coal (for hundreds of years) and pretty much, also, in natural gas. The problem is oil, 42% of which we have to import now, and which we will still be heavily importing by 2020, no matter what we do. Romney could propose an *eventual* solution to our lack of independence in oil that could be well along by 2020, but so far, he hasn't.

The only solution to the oil problem that the Republicans have proposed involves more drilling for oil in this country, and that will not solve the problem, no matter how hard they try. Romney made a vague reference to "renewables" but provided no specifics. Here, specifically, is what he needs to propose:

1. The U. S. should begin a large scale effort to shift, not to battery powered cars, but to hydrogen powered cars.

2. This involves a large scale effort to produce hydrogen *from water*, all of which is H2O and can be river water, sea water, etc.

3. It will take a lot of electric power which can be produced by wind turbines. The electric power is used to separate the water into its two components, hydrogen

and oxygen (the oxygen is also useful, of course).

4. The hydrogen is in the form of a gas which can be shipped from place to place by pipeline, railroad tank cars, etc. The hydrogen for cars can be sold in small tanks, or can be dispensed from pumps similar to those used for gasoline (from oil) at the present time.

5. The hydrogen powered cars can be very similar to the gasoline powered cars we use at the present time. They can have internal combustion engines similar to the ones we use now, or they can use fuel cells, which are difficult and expensive to produce at the present time.

6. The point is, hydrogen from water has no carbon and therefore does not pollute the atmosphere and cause global warming. Also, since water covers about 70% of the earth, hydrogen from water can be produced in unlimited quantities and can be substituted, effectively, for gasoline made from oil, in virtually all applications—aviation

> being a possible exception. Thus, by using hydrogen from water, we can achieve energy independence in oil, perhaps not by 2020, but certainly by some time this century.

Romney could propose this, as outlined above; the question is, will he? Does he have the vision to do more than propose energy independence for North America?

Romney lost the election, not because he lacked the vision to do more with respect to energy independence, but because of other failings, and so we are left with President Obama for an additional four year term. I have serious doubt that he will do anything about my hydrogen proposals, either.

The truth about Energy Independence is that we can accomplish it by switching, from oil to hydrogen. We can try to accomplish it some other way, but we will ***fail*** if we try to accomplish it some other way. The quantities involved are simply immense. The sooner we get started, the sooner we will accomplish our goal, if Energy Independence is our goal.

There are three significant considerations that favor the use of pure hydrogen, made from water, as a means of restoring our Energy Independence, rather than by trying to do it some other way.

FIRST: Pure hydrogen can be made from water in unlimited quantities, right here in the U. S. Hydrogen makes up 75 per cent, or more, of all the matter in the entire universe. It is the stuff from which the stars, including our sun, is made.

SECOND: Pure hydrogen, made from water, is totally non-polluting. By switching to hydrogen, we will eliminate the U. S. contribution to the global warming problem, because hydrogen production can be totally carbon-free, as I have described. Thus, every dollar invested in hydrogen production, and usage, will also go to solving the global warming/climate change problem.

THIRD: At some future time, fuel cell cars may become practical. If and when we begin the switch to fuel cell cars, we will have the pure hydrogen fuel in place. You need to be aware of the fact that fuel cell cars will ***require*** pure hydrogen, made from water; that's the ***only*** fuel that fuel cell cars will run on. That is, fuel cell cars won't run on gasoline, or ethanol, or anything else; just pure hydrogen, made from water.

At this point, I need to back up a little. I said, earlier, that the United States can never again achieve energy independence in terms of oil, and then I began talking about substituting hydrogen for oil. I suspect that most of you believe that we **can** achieve energy independence in terms of oil. If the U. S. just takes off the restrictions on oil drilling in this country, we can drill our way out of this problem. At least, that's what many Republicans believe, or want to believe.

I don't want to be the bearer of bad tidings. I would like to be able to tell you that, yes, we can do it. We can achieve energy independence in terms of oil, just as Mitt Romney was promising. But I have to tell you the truth. It's impossible. Even Romney knew that U. S. energy independence in terms of oil was an impossible goal. When he proposed North American energy independence in terms of oil, that wasn't a slip of the tongue. He really did intend to include *Canadian oil* in his proposal, even though, as president of the United States, he would obviously have no control of *Canadian oil*, as I was pointing out. Canada is the biggest foreign oil supplier to the U. S. And Canada is obviously the friendliest foreign oil supplier to the U. S. We all hope, and assume, that friendly relationship will continue. It is assumed that Canada will continue to accept the U. S. dollar in payment for all of the Canadian oil that we are importing.

But that brings me to this important point about importing oil. We have to **pay** for the oil we import, whether we get it from Canada or from some other country. The whole notion of having to pay for imported oil affects the concept of U. S. energy independence. To the extent we have to import oil, we are **not** energy independent in terms of oil.

The reason the U. S. became a net oil importer, immediately after the conclusion of World War II, was that the foreign oil was cheaper than the U. S. oil it replaced. We have not been energy independent, in terms of oil, since that time. And, since that time, the U. S. has become dependent on the imported oil, because U. S. oil consumption quickly outpaced U.S. oil production, in the years since World War II. Imported oil became a necessity for the U. S. economy to function as it has, since the war. I want to make this point clear, beyond any doubt. The United States cannot, ***ever***, become energy independent in terms of oil. It isn't just because we can't become energy independent in terms of oil by increasing our domestic production. With the restrictions off, there is no doubt that we can somewhat increase our domestic oil production, at least for awhile.

But the real problem is one of **cost.** No matter what we do, the cheap oil is gone **forever,** used up, and the oil we have left is going to be very expensive to produce. Right now, we're enjoying production from an immense oil pool, from miles underground, in North Dakota. But it's not cheap oil.

Increasingly, the U. S. taxpayer will have to subsidize U. S. oil production, and there is no indication that the U. S. taxpayer is going to be willing to, or even able to, subsidize domestic oil production, year in and year out.

So ultimately, COST is the reason why the United States cannot become energy independent in terms of OIL. It is IMPOSSIBLE!

But now for the good news. There **is** a way that the United States can become truly energy independent, now and forever!

Before I tell you how, I need to caution you. You may believe you know how, and may therefore be inclined to tune me out. Please don't tune me out. Instead, trust me.

The answer is: HYDROGEN. Pure hydrogen. Hydrogen made from WATER, H-2-O.

Let me explain a little. We have been using hydrogen all along. All of the "fossil fuels" that we have been using as energy sources . . . coal, oil, natural gas . . . contain hydrogen. We call these "fossil fuels" by another name. We call them HYDROCARBONS. They are made, primarily, from hydrogen and carbon.

These "fossil fuels" . . . these hydrocarbons . . . were made from natural sources, here on earth, and were stored underground, millions and millions of years ago. We've been bringing them up, through mining and drilling, and have been using them.

We've been burning them, and in doing so, we now find that we have been polluting the atmosphere with the carbon, contributing to the "greenhouse effect" that causes the atmosphere to retain heat. This appears to be the cause of the unusual degree of "global warming" that we have lately been hearing so much about. We don't get global warming from burning pure hydrogen, made from water. And we don't get any global warming when we make hydrogen from water, if we do it right.

Every school child learns that water is H-2-O. Water is a combination of oxygen and hydrogen. Chemists refer to water as a compound, made up of hydrogen and oxygen, tightly bonded together. Hydrogen and oxygen are both gases. They are tasteless, odorless, and non-toxic. Both are part of the air we breathe. They are part of all of us. Scientists tell us that the human body is about 60 to 70 per cent water. Which means that the human body is largely made up of hydrogen and oxygen. We humans must have oxygen in order to live, and we humans are not equipped with gills as fish are, which means we can't derive our oxygen from water as fish can. We have to get our oxygen from the "air," which is mostly nitrogen but has enough oxygen in it for our needs. (If we go above 15,000 feet above sea level, we have to have supplementary oxygen.)

Now I want to talk briefly about hydrogen, and how we can make it from water. To make hydrogen from water, we run an electric current through the water. This is direct current, the kind we could get from a battery. We collect the bubbles of hydrogen at one pole, and we collect the bubbles of oxygen at the other pole. These are gas bubbles, and we store the hydrogen bubbles in one container, and the oxygen bubbles in another container. Both have their uses.

We compress the hydrogen bubbles so that we can hold more hydrogen gas in the container. We need a pretty strong container to hold the compressed hydrogen gas. At ordinary temperatures, we need to use a container that is strong enough to withstand a pressure of anywhere between one-thousand and ten-thousand pounds per square inch, which we refer to as p.s.i. The container needs to be made of steel or of some very strong plastic.

This process, whereby we make pure hydrogen from water by using electricity to break the very strong bond between hydrogen and oxygen that makes up the liquid compound that we call water, has a name. The name of the process is electrolysis.

And by the way, there is nothing new about this process of electrolysis. Electrolysis is a natural process that has been known for about 200 years. Experimenters discovered that running an electric current through water could cause the water to separate into its two components, hydrogen and oxygen. WARNING! Do NOT try electrolysis at home!

Hydrogen is an explosive gas. It is said to be a "more energy intense fuel" than gasoline. A kilogram of hydrogen--that's one-thousand grams--has about the same energy as a gallon of gasoline.

Now here's where it gets interesting. The process of electrolysis can, essentially, be reversed, in a device known as a fuel cell. The resulting electrical energy can then be used to run an electric motor which can be used to power an automobile.

The auto manufacturers have been working on fuel cell cars for many years. All of the auto companies have experimental fuel cell cars on the road, but that's what they are so far, experimental. The fuel cells are very costly to produce, and they don't last very long. At some future time, fuel cell cars may become available for all of us to drive, but there is no telling when that might be.

If and when fuel cell cars become available, they will need hydrogen made from water to run on. In the meantime, however, we can burn hydrogen in ordinary internal combustion engines, slightly modified, much like we do gasoline.

"Burned in an internal-combustion engine, hydrogen produces nearly three times the energy as the same weight of gasoline . . . " That's a direct quote from a book titled *The End of Oil*, by Paul Roberts. The Federal government has been producing hydrogen from water for years, at the National Renewable Energy Laboratory, located at Golden, Colorado, (near Denver,) part of the U. S. Department of Energy, using essentially off-the-shelf equipment.

Ford Motor Company has actually produced, and sold, vehicles powered by internal combustion engines that have been modified to efficiently "burn" hydrogen. It's important to realize that these are **not** fuel cell vehicles; typically, they are vans that run in the limited areas of the country where hydrogen to power them is readily available.

What modifications are necessary in order to make an ordinary, internal-combustion engine burn hydrogen instead of gasoline? Here's what Ford Motor Company engineers said they installed:

- fuel injectors designed specifically for hydrogen
- high-compression pistons
- a coil-on-plug ignition system
- an electronic throttle
- new engine management software

But that's about it. So, this is how we achieve energy independence. We make hydrogen. That's pure hydrogen, made from water. We do this entirely here in the U. S. A. We thus replace imported oil with domestically produced hydrogen, made from water.

Where do we get the water? From our big rivers, such as the Mississippi. Or from the oceans. Water is water. We need electricity, in order to make hydrogen via electrolysis. We could get the electricity from our regular power grid. But in order to get it, pollution-free, we should get it from wind turbines. Or from solar cells. Or from nuclear power plants. We need to get the electric power cheaply, so that the hydrogen will be cheap; wind turbines may be the best answer.

One of the neat things about hydrogen is supply. We can make as much hydrogen as we want. In other words, we can have an unlimited supply of hydrogen, made from water, a "free" resource, using wind power, another "free" resource.

We can power our cars with hydrogen. We can power our trucks and buses with hydrogen. We can use hydrogen to generate electricity. By using hydrogen, made from water, we can become energy independent. And, since water, and hydrogen, and oxygen, are all totally carbon free, we also solve the global warming problem.

In fact, the sooner we switch to pure hydrogen, made from water, the sooner we stop injecting greenhouse gases into the atmosphere. And we then show the rest of the world how to do it. We provide the leadership, and the technology.

Switching to pure hydrogen, made from water, is the way the United States can become energy independent, now and forever. That's why hydrogen is sometimes referred to as the "forever fuel."

I don't want to leave you with the impression that switching to hydrogen can be easily done. There are a lot of deniers and naysayers. There are a lot of vested interests to overcome. Money and jobs are at stake. It is going to take time to accomplish. Substantial investment will be required.

However, it is clear that hydrogen, from water, is the most practical alternative fuel for a number of reasons, one of which is supply. We can make an unlimited supply of hydrogen from water, simply because water recycles, and about 70 per cent of the earth's surface is covered by water. Hydrogen from water does not cause pollution and does not need to contribute to global warming.

The best thing to do with hydrocarbons is, leave them in the ground. Don't burn them and then try to inject the carbon back into the ground.

Switching completely to hydrogen will have to take place over a period best measured in decades. Thus, there is plenty of time for existing interests using petroleum to be gradually phased out. There is no need to convert all energy use to hydrogen; in fact, aviation should continue to use petroleum and should not use hydrogen, for practical reasons (except for big rockets, which use extremely cold, ***liquid*** hydrogen).

We will need new automobiles, designed for use with hydrogen. At the present time, they will be equipped with internal combustion engines, modified for efficient use of hydrogen. They should cost about the same as the autos we now use, powered by gasoline, made from petroleum.

Fuel cell cars may be practical, at some time in the future, but they are much too costly to manufacture and maintain, at the present time. Auto manufacturers have been promising mass production of fuel cell cars for years, but this has been based more on hype and hope than on reality.

I have proposed that hydrogen powered cars be equipped with on-board fuel tanks ***and*** also with the capability of using hydrogen sold in small, portable tanks that can be distributed by existing convenience stores, obviating the need for any elaborate infrastructure for pumping hydrogen into cars. The small tanks could be of a uniform size and would be returnable and refillable. (Recall that it wasn't long ago that milk was sold in returnable and refillable bottles. This was done for decades.)

It is probably going to require some action or commitment by the Federal government to get the switchover to hydrogen started. The impetus may come from the need to reduce the level of carbon pollution of the earth's atmosphere. Hydrogen from water would seem to be the obvious answer, but no one is pushing for hydrogen, while a considerable effort is being made to push for the use of natural gas, which can reduce carbon pollution but not eliminate it totally, as hydrogen from water can do. I think the use of natural gas simply delays the inevitable use of hydrogen from water and therefore am opposed to the temporary expedient that natural gas producers are proposing.

The focus of the above discussion is on the automobile. But there is another aspect to the future use of hydrogen that I want to mention. At the present time, enviornmental organizations such as the Sierra Club, and the U. S. government's Environmental Protection Agency, are working to reduce the use of "dirty" energy souces by electric utility companies. Coal is the biggest factor in U. S. electric generation at the present time, and is considered to be the biggest polluter. Therefore, the present emphasis is on moving the electric utilities away from the use of coal.

There is no such thing as "clean coal." It is possible to "scrub" coal and make it cleaner burning than it would be otherwise, but it is not possible to rid coal of carbon, which is the big pollutant in terms of the earth's atmosphere.

Thus, at the present time, the EPA and the Sierra Club are trying to get utilities to abandon the use of coal altogether.

Mid-American Energy is a big midwestern electric utility that has gone heavily into wind generation, with nearly a third of its generating capacity now coming from hundreds of wind turbines. But pressed to give up on coal, Mid-American is considering a big nuclear plant. In a February 24, 2013 editorial, the Des Moines *Register* raised questions about Mid-American's future energy choices, saying that wind "can't be counted on for base load capacity because the wind doesn't always blow when power is needed." I couldn't resist writing a Letter to the Editor in which I pointed out that "wind power can be stored, and used when the wind isn't blowing."

> How? By using wind-generated electricity to make hydrogen from water (think river water) and then "burning" the stored hydrogen to generate electricity when needed. Pure hydrogen, made from water, has no carbon and therefore does not pollute our atmosphere and cause

> global warming. And we can "make" an unlimited supply of hydrogen from water. Furthermore, hydrogen can also substitute for natural gas. Finally, Mid-American can make extra revenue from the sale of any excess hydrogen and from the sale of oxygen it will produce as it splits water into its two components, hydrogen and oxygen.

What I had in mind, of course, was the fact that an electric utility like Mid-American Energy Company could be a supplier of hydrogen for our cars, in the future. It would be a natural outgrowth of producing pure hydrogen, from water, for its own use. The water could come from the great rivers of the midwest, two of which flank the State of Iowa, already a major factor in wind energy production. With water from the Mississippi and the Missouri, Iowa is well-positioned for the production of hydrogen, as it is now producing huge quantities of ethanol. And just to the northwest lies North Dakota, rapidly becoming a major oil producer, and with great wind energy potential. Both Iowa and North Dakota neighbor with Minnesota, with thousands of lakes and bordering on Lake

Superior, and with South Dakota, through which the Missouri River passes and also with wind potential. This group of States also is served by major transcontinental railroads and interstate highways.

I see this group of States beginning the large scale production of hydrogen, from water, using wind energy to produce the electricity needed to separate the water into its components: hydrogen and oxygen. Eventually, we are going to be forced to turn our energy economy away from hydrocarbons toward a fuel that contains no carbon. That fuel is hydrogen, made from water. It's only a matter of time before the carbon pollution threat drives us in this direction. Mid-American Energy is the type of company that can provide the necessary leadership.

EPILOGUE

James Madison was elected to the House of Representatives, and from that position, was able to work for adoption of the Bill of Rights that now forms such an important part of our Constitution.

In proposing a Second Bill of Rights, as I have done in this book, I am dependent upon members of Congress both to introduce the amendments I have drafted and to work for their passage. I am well aware of the fact that this is probably going to be a very difficult job, because it involves changing, and modernizing, what the Framers did.

However, it is not impossible. Readers of this book can get it done, if enough of them feel that doing it is worthwhile.

For example, millions of Americans are heavily dependent on Social Security and Medicare. Their votes had a lot to do with the outcome of the 2012 presidential election. Two of my proposed Constitutional Amendments, numbers four and five, are aimed at making Social

Security and Medicare permanent. Congress must not be allowed to treat Social Security and Medicare as "entitlements" to be reduced or eliminated. These are programs for which present beneficiaries have paid, over the years, and for which future beneficiaries are making their contributions now. Congress has no moral right to take them away, and it is high time that Social Security, and Medicare, are protected by making them part of the U. S. Constitution.

Also very important is my proposal Number Three, a Balanced Budget Amendment that will really work to stop deficit spending by Congress and put the United States government on a sound financial footing. My proposal for a Balanced Budget Amendment was mostly written about 25 years ago and is much better than any of the proposals that Congress has considered in the past. Why is it better?

- Because it fixes the mistake the Founding Fathers made in the original Constitution, in giving Congress the unlimited power to borrow money on the credit of the United States, without establishing any duty to pay it back within a reasonable time.

- Because it provides a revenue source in the form of a ***limited*** retail sales tax that allows Congress to start using a balanced budget immediately rather than running up more debt.

- Because it prevents Congress from easily voting to override it, yet establishes a realistic procedure for allowing emergency deficit spending to take place if the nation is faced with a true emergency.

- Because it gives the president a limited item veto authority over any excessive spending by Congress, yet allows Congress to do what Congress really needs to do.

Of course, I am not completely dependent on other members of Congress to introduce my amendment proposals. I am running for Congress, again, myself. However, just getting these amendment proposals introduced, in Congress, is a long way from getting them passed (by a two-thirds vote in both the House and the Senate) and then getting them ratified, by 38 States.

So, as a practical matter, I will need a lot of help. In Congress. And in the state legislatures. And by the citizens of the United States. By making these proposed constitutional amendments available in book form, both as conventional paper books and as e-books, I am giving the American people some ideas as to what I think needs to be done, soon.

All twelve of the proposed amendments set forth in Section One of this book need to be adopted, as soon as possible. This could be done within a matter of months. In my view, all twelve of the amendment proposals in Section One are of about equal importance; that's why I think they should all be introduced, and passed by Congress, immediately. They are intended to solve immediate problems. If I were to identify any one of them as most important, I would say that proposal Number Three is most important: a balanced budget amendment that will really work, to stop deficit spending ***and*** to put the United States government on a sound financial footing for the future.

All of the urgent maneuvering over how much to raise the marginal income tax rates on the "richest" American taxpayers involved only enough money with which to run the government for a few days, at best. The big elephant in the room was over what to do about the fact that Congress was spending about a trillion dollars a year more than the government was taking in, an obviously unsustainable situation.

No amount of economizing is going to bridge a gap of that magnitude. It is going to take an entirely new revenue source, and that's where my national retail sales tax proposal, included in my balanced budget amendment (proposal Number Three) comes in.

No one is going to put up with the income tax increase that would be necessary to balance the Federal budget. The retail sales tax has several advantages, including the fact that it would be largely self-imposed. With all of the exemptions in section 8 of proposal Number Three, and by exemption of the first $10,000 of an automobile purchase, what's left would be a tolerable amount of tax for any individual to pay. Obviously, the affluent would pay more, but only if they were buying goods. If they saved their money, bought stocks, real estate, etc., they wouldn't be paying the sales tax. On February 22, 2013, the *New York Times* ran an editorial titled "Why Taxes Have to Go Up." Here's how it started out:

> Democrats and Republicans remain at odds on how to avoid a round of budget cuts so deep and arbitrary that to allow them now could push the economy back into recession. . . . To reduce the deficit in a weak economy, new taxes on high-income Americans are a matter of necessity and fairness; they are also a necessary precondition to what in time will have to be tax increases on the middle class.

The *Times* editorial then went on to try to justify higher income taxes on high earners as "a needed step" prior to imposing higher income taxes "from further down the income scale." The editorial was then followed, on the internet version, with about 500 comments, most of which were bitterly opposed to what the *Times* was proposing. In fact, the comments were exactly along the lines that I predicted, above;

the people are just not going to put up with such increases in the income tax.

I made an on-line comment as follows; this is the exact text of my comment as it was "published" in the web edition of the *New York Times*:

> All six members of Iowa's congressional delegation have the solution in their hands at the present time. It is my version of a balance-the-budget amendment to the U. S. Constitution that includes authorization for a national retail sales tax with exemptions that practically eliminate regressive tendencies normally associated with sales taxes. It is limited to 50% of spending and therefore augments, rather than replaces, the income tax as the federal government's primary revenue source. Congress is authorized to create further exemptions; thus, I suggest a $10,000 exemption on automobile purchases. Other amendments in the package I submitted would remove Social Security and Medicare from the

> Federal budget altogether. I call my 12 amendment proposals a Second Bill of Rights, intended to reform and modernize the U. S. Constitution. They do NOT replace the original Bill of Rights. They are all set forth, and explained, in the Second, Revised edition of my book Meltdown! that will be published in March or early April by iUniverse.

Retail sales taxes are imposed by most state governments and by some local governments. They are familiar to most people in this country, and are obviously tolerable by most of us. They are relatively simple to pay, and simple to collect. A national retail sales tax on goods is the most practical way to provide the Federal government with the revenue needed to stop further borrowing by the Federal government. My proposal Number Three could be quickly adopted, and implemented, and Congress would be forced to stop borrowing.

Many people will shrink back from the retail sales tax idea. I understand that reaction perfectly well, but it's one of those things that just has to be done. It's a tool, a method for balancing the budget; in fact, when I originally proposed it, in my book *Great Restraint,* published back in 1986, I thought of it as just a budget-balancer.

But now, it is a vital necessity. We ***must*** stop spending a trillion dollars a year more than we are taking in. We ***can't*** get that by just raising the income tax, and we ***can't*** cut spending by a trillion dollars a year.

So, we have to have another, large source of revenue. Now. A trillion dollars a year. We can get it from the sales tax.

This doesn't need to be forever. Over time, we can trim Federal spending in any of a variety of ways. We can make various adjustments.

But right now, we have to balance our budget. Start with my balance-the-budget amendment. Authorize the sales tax. We will all feel better for having gotten things under control. We can then consider what adjustments in spending, and in taxation, that we want to make. We can make the necessary adjustments, secure in the knowledge that our children will inherit the great country we have, the United States of America.

We can make Social Security, and Medicare, permanent. We can secure our constitutional rights by setting up the National Court of Appeals. We can abolish the doctrine of sovereign immunity. We can make it clear that we will meet our national financial obligations by adopting my "no default" amendment. We can abolish the mandate to buy health insurance, and adopt some other method (such as the one I suggested in Number Nine) to make medical care available to those who don't have health insurance. We can adopt reasonable term limits for members of Congress. We can restore the right of the people to propose amendments to the U. S. Constitution, the way the Framers of the Constitution intended. And we can require Congress to conduct our nation's governmental business in an efficient manner, free from silly rules with which Congress itself struggles, unable to free itself, by adopting my proposed amendment Number Twelve.

Let the ideas in this book be your guide. You can get a copy of it, the whole thing, for $3.99 or less, for your Kindle, Nook, or other e-reader. Or get a paper copy, for a little more. Read it. Discuss it with your friends and neighbors. You don't have to agree with all of it. But you can use it as a starting point.

Get your Congress person to introduce the twelve proposed amendments in Section One so as to begin the process needed to bring about the changes that you ***know*** are needed.

Certainly the proposals in Section Two are worth considering. And the ideas in Section Three are worth discussing also. But the most critical ideas are in Section One. Get those established as soon as possible, within the next few months. It is possible to amend the U. S. Constitution within a few months. That's all it took to pass the original Bill of Rights, at a time that communication instantaneously was impossible, something that most of you do, every day, without giving it a moment's thought.

You don't need to be arrogant. Just insistent. Your Congress person may try to ignore you. So, get together with some of your friends, and insist. If your Congress person continues to ignore you, get some more of your friends and neighbors to help. At some point, your Congress person will begin to realize that you mean business.

I want to take just a minute to tell you about what happened when I sent all twelve of the amendment proposals, via FAX, to the six members of the Iowa congressional delegation. In each case, my transmission was accompanied by an individualized covering letter.

To Senator Charles Grassley, FAX number (202) 224-6020, sent Jan. 25, 2013.

To Senator Tom Harkin, FAX number (202) 224-9369, sent Jan. 25, 2013.

To Representative Tom Latham, FAX number (202) 225-3301, sent Jan. 26, 2013.

To Representative Bruce Braley, FAX number (202) 225-6666, sent Feb. 5, 2013.

To Representative Steve King, FAX number (202) 225-3193, sent Feb. 5, 2013.

To Representative Dave Loebsack, FAX number (202) 226-0757, sent Feb. 5, 2013.

In each case, in my covering letter, I described this book and said: “If you introduce these amendments soon, I will note that fact in the book. If you don't, that fact also will be noted." I asked them for both their consideration and their cooperation.

So, what happened? Nothing. Absolutely nothing. In fact, by May of 2013, when I was transmitting my computer files of the completed manuscript of this book to iUniverse, not one of the members of the Iowa congressional delegation to whom I had sent the initial twelve amendment proposals had even acknowledged receipt of my FAX transmission. NOT ONE WORD! This is exactly what I expected.

It is going to take a very determined effort to get Congress to officially "propose" these amendments to the U. S. Constitution.

What you want is to get these proposed amendments introduced, in both houses of Congress. If they have already been introduced, you want to get your Congress persons to join in sponsoring the amendment proposals. And then, just keep going. Eventually, it is going to take a favorable vote, by a two-thirds margin, in ***both*** houses of the U. S. Congress, in order to officially "propose" these amendments.

At that point, the proposed amendments are sent to the State legislatures of all of the States. It takes a favorable vote in both houses of your State legislature (just one, if you're in Nebraska). Once the legislatures in thirty-eight states have approved (ratified) the amendments that Congress has officially "proposed," you have achieved success.

But wait. You're not done yet. Congress then has to act to pass the legislation that will be necessary to implement the various amendments. If you have gotten this far, however, the rest is relatively easy, and relatively routine. All of the amendments in Section One, with the possible exception of Number Two, will require legislation in order to make the policy changes that the proposed amendments are aimed at accomplishing. This will not be an overnight task, but you'll just have to keep on insisting, and Congress, and the President, will eventually get it done. You'll just have to be a little patient.

The hard part is getting the amendment proposals adopted. The relatively easy part is getting them implemented. You and your friends can get it done. I can't do it. I wrote the book, but you and your friends will have to get it done. I wish success, to all of you.

Paul D. Lunde

Photographs

Giant wind turbines like this one, located just north of the town of Blairsburg, Iowa, are being erected all over the United States by electric utility companies, eager to add pollution-free generating capacity. The same kind of wind turbines can be used to generate the electric current needed to produce hydrogen from water by means of electrolysis. A cluster of these turbines could be grouped around a hydrogen (and oxygen) production facility. Refillable containers of hydrogen could be transported by truck or rail to existing gas stations and convenience stores.

My point is that there is no need for an elaborate and expensive hydrogen distribution system to be built prior to putting hydrogen-powered motor vehicles on the road, if the vehicles themselves are properly built to use the refillable containers in the first place. On the next page, I'll show you how hydrogen fuel for motor vehicles can be distributed without first building a system of pipelines; the pipelines can be built later.

Also, there are practical reasons for using the refillable containers for hydrogen fuel. I'm not at all sure that self-service pumps for hydrogen are going to be practical, but that doesn't mean we shouldn't use hydrogen to power our motor vehicles.

This convenience store has no pump for hydrogen gas. In fact, there is no need for such a pump. Notice the rack with propane gas containers next to the building, near the center of the picture. A similar rack could be used for the sale of hydrogen, in refillable containers. The hydrogen containers could simply be inserted in the "ports" with which hydrogen-powered vehicles should be equipped.

A closeup picture of the metal rack containing propane gas for sale by this convenience store shows the method by which stores such as this one could sell hydrogen fuel to motorists. In the beginning, at least, consumers may prefer to buy their hydrogen in the refillable containers, permitting quick refueling, rather than waiting in a line to use the single hydrogen pump that many service stations may try to get by with, when hydrogen-powered vehicles are still a novelty.

Select Bibliography

BOOKS

Black, Edwin, *Internal Combustion* (New York: St. Martin's Press, 2006)

Bowen, Catherine Drinker, *Miracle at Philadelphia* (Boston: Atlantic Monthly Press/Little, Brown and Co. paperback, 1966)

Cullop, Floyd G., *The Constitution of the United States* (New York: Mentor paperback, 1983)

Edel, Wilbur, *A Constitutional Convention: Threat or Challenge?* (New York: Praeger Publishers, 1981)

Deffeyes, Kenneth S., *Beyond Oil* (New York: Hill and Wang, 2005)

Freund, Paul A.; Sutherland, Arthur E.; Howe, Mark De Wolfe; and Brown, Ernest J., *Constitutional Law* (Boston: Little, Brown and Co., 1954)

Gingrich, Newt, with Halby, Vince, *Drill Here, Drill Now, Pay Less* (Washington: Regnery Publishing, Inc. paperback, 2008)

Hamilton, Alexander; Madison, James; and Jay, John, *The Federalist Papers* (New York: Mentor paperback, 1961)

Kunstler, James Howard, *The Long Emergency* (New York: Grove Press paperback, 2005)

Levy, Leonard W., *Origins of the Bill of Rights* (New Haven: Yale University Press paperback, 1999)

Rifkin, Jeremy, *The Hydrogen Economy* (New York: Jeremy P. Tarcher/Penguin paperback, 2002)

Roberts, Paul, *The End of Oil* (Boston, New York: Houghton Mifflin Company, 2004)

Roston, Eric, *The Carbon Age* (New York: Walker and Company, 2008)

Sampson, Anthony, *The Seven Sisters* (New York: Bantam Books paperback, 1975)

Sandalow, David, *Freedom from Oil* (New York: McGraw-Hill, 2008)

Smith, Edward Conrad, editor, *The Constitution of the United States* (New York: Barnes & Noble, paperback, 1979)

Smith, Page, *The Constitution: A Documentary and Narrative History* (New York: William Morrow and Company, Inc., 1978)

Tertzakian, Peter, *A Thousand Barrels a Second* (New York: McGraw-Hill, 2006)

Tuchman, Barbara W., *The Zimmermann Telegram* (New York: Ballantine Books, paperback, 1958, 1966)

ARTICLES

Ashley, Steven, "*On the Road to Fuel-Cell Cars,*" Scientific American, March, 2005, pp. 62-69.

Gottfried, Kurt; Kendall, Henry W.; Lee, John M. , "*'No First Use' of Nuclear Weapons,*" Scientific American, Mar., 1984, pp. 33-41.

King, Ralph, *"Mary Tolan's Modest Proposal,"* Business, June, 2003, pp. 116-122.

Lambert, Craig, *"The Hydrogen-Powered Future,"* Harvard Magazine, January-February, 2004, pp. 30-35, 92-95.

Ogden, Joan, *"High Hopes for Hydrogen,"* Scientific American, September, 2006, pp. 94-101.

Parfit, Michel, *"Future Power,"* National Geographic, August, 2005, pp. 2-31.

Pinkerton, Frederick E., and Wicke, Brian G., *"Bottling the Hydrogen Genie,"* The Industrial Physicist, February/March, 2004, pp. 20-23.

Weiler, Lawrence D., *"No First Use:a History,"* Bulletin of the Atomic Scientists, Feb. 1983, pp. 28-34.

Chapter Notes

SECTION ONE

Number One: Choosing the Electors and Supporting Article: The 2000 Supreme Court case that finally “settled” the presidential election that year is *Bush v. Gore*, 531 U.S. 98, 121 S.Ct. 525, 148 L.Ed.2d 388 (2000).

Number Two: The American Traditions and Supporting Article.

Number Three: The Balance the Budget Constitutional Amendment and Supporting Article. The 1880 Supreme Court case that decided a Federal income tax was not a “direct tax” and therefore did not violate the constitutional prohibition was *Springer v. United States*, 102 U. S. 586, 26 L.Ed. 253 (1880). The 1895 Supreme Court case that went the other way, in a 5-4 decision, was *Pollack v. Farmers' Loan & Trust Co.*, 157 U. S. 429, 15 S.Ct. 673, 39 L.Ed. 759 (1895), *affirmed on rehearing,* 158 U. S. 601, 15 S.Ct. 912, 39 L.Ed. 1108 (1895).

Obviously, this was a very controversial decision by the U. S. Supreme Court, and it led directly to the Sixteenth Amendment of the U. S. Constitution, which was officially proposed by Congress in 1909, and finally ratified by the State Legislatures in 1913, just prior to the outbreak of World War I in Europe. (The United States, of course, did not officially get involved in World War I until 1917, following discovery of the "Zimmermann Telegram," which revealed German perfidy beyond what even President Woodrow Wilson could put up with, and he asked Congress to declare war, which it very promptly did. The rest is history.) Long after adoption of the Sixteenth Amendment, the Supreme Court overturned one aspect of the *Pollack* decision in *South Carolina v. Baker,* 485 U. S. 505, 108 S.Ct. 1355, 99 L.Ed.2d 592 (1988).

Number Four: Making Social Security Permanent and Supporting Article.

Number Five: Making Medicare Permanent and Supporting Article.

Number Six: Establishing the National Court of Appeals and Supporting Article: The famous Supreme Court school desegregation case that I referred to in the Supporting Article is *Brown v. Board of Education,* 347 U. S. 483, 74 S.Ct. 686, 98 L.Ed. 873 (1954). The Fourteenth Amendment to the U. S. Constitution, Section 1, second sentence, upon which the *Brown* case is based, says:

> "No State shall make or enforce any law which shall abridge the privileges or immunities of citizens of the United States; **nor shall any State deprive any person of life, liberty, or property, without due process of law; nor deny to any person within its jurisdiction the equal protection of the laws." [Emphasis supplied.]**

One of the laws passed by Congress to enforce the 14th Amendment, §1, is this one, 42 U. S. Code Section 1983:

> "Every **person** who, under color of any statute, ordinance, regulation, custom, or usage, of any State or Territory or the District of Columbia, subjects, or causes to be subjected,

> any citizen of the United States or other person within the jurisdiction thereof to the deprivation of any rights, privileges, or immunities secured by the Constitution and laws, shall be liable to the party injured in an action at law, suit in equity, or other proper proceeding for redress..."

In one of the cases I told you about, I was suing a State official because the State itself was immune from suit [see my Number Seven on sovereign immunity]; the State official was obviously a person. But I knew that the Supreme Court had ruled that a State official was not a person! That ruling was in a 1989 case, *Will v. Michigan Dept. of State Police*, 491 U. S. 58, 109 S.Ct. 2304, 105 L.Ed. 45. Because of this ruling, I could not sue under 42 U.S.C. §1983, and because I didn't sue under §1983, the District Court judge dismissed my case and the Eighth Circuit affirmed him because **they** had ruled that I could not sue directly under the 14th Amendment but I had to use §1983, and when I went to the Supreme Court, the answer was "*certiorari denied*" and so it was back to the District Court for another try. . . There really isn't any question about it; we need a National Court of Appeals, and as I show in Number Seven, we need to abolish the obviously obsolete doctrine of sovereign immunity because **that** was the reason why the Supreme Court in *Will* had ruled that a State **official** (obviously a person, as the Supreme Court acknowledged) was **not** a person for purposes of 42 U. S. Code §1983!

Number Seven: Abolishing the Doctrine of Sovereign Immunity and Supporting Article: The citation for the 1890 Supreme Court case that, as a practical matter, put sovereign immunity **back** into the U. S. Constitution is *Hans v. Louisiana,* 134 U.S. 1, 101 S.Ct. 504, 33 L.Ed. 842 (1890). The contortions that the Supreme Court engages in, to try to justify its continued adherance to the doctrine of sovereign immunity, are perfectly illustrated in the case of *Kimel v. Florida Bd. of Regents,* 528 U. S. 62, 120 S.Ct. 631, 145 L.Ed.2d 522 (2000). The need, for my proposal Number Seven, is obvious.

Number Eight: No Default and Supporting Article.

Number Nine: No Mandate to Buy Health Insurance and Supporting Article: The Supreme Court case that upheld the Obamacare law is *National Federation of Independent Business v. Sebelius,* 5__ U. S. ____, 132 S. Ct. 2566, 183 L.Ed.2d 450 (2012). Incidentally, the opinions of the various justices in this important case ran more than 100 pages. This explains why the Supreme Court simply does not have time to handle the ordinary person's case, and why we need the National Court of Appeals (see my Number Six, above), so that the ordinary person can have the quality of justice that the Founding Fathers intended for all of us to have!

Number Ten: Term Limits for Congress and Supporting Article: The Supreme Court case that turned down State attempts to apply term limits to Congress is *U. S. Term Limits, Inc. v.Thornton*, 514 U. S. 779, 115 S.Ct. 1842, 131 L.Ed.2d 881 (1995).

Number Eleven: Amending to Amend and Supporting Article.

Number Twelve: Congressional Rules and Supporting Article.

SECTION TWO

Number Thirteen: Financing Federal Election Campaigns and Supporting Article: The Supreme Court case that invalidated efforts by Congress to limit corporate spending in political campaigns is *Citizens United v. Federal Election Com'n.,* 558 U. S. 310, 130 S.Ct. 876, 175 L.Ed.2d 753 (2010).

Number Fourteen: Restricting Mortgage Foreclosures and Supporting Article.

Number Fifteen: Immigration Reform and Supporting Article.

Number Sixteen: Let Them Run and Supporting Article.

Number Seventeen: No First Use of Nuclear Weapons and Supporting Article.

SECTION THREE

A Grading System for the Twenty-First Century.

Airports for the Twenty-First Century.

A Woman's Right to Choose: The Supreme Court case that established abortion as a constitutional right is *Roe v. Wade,* 410 U. S. 113, 93 S.Ct. 705, 35 L.Ed.2d 147 (1973). The more recent case I mentioned is *Gonzales v. Carhart,* 550 U. S. 124, 127 S.Ct. 1610, 167 L.Ed.2d 480 (2007).

The Truth About Energy Independence.

EPILOGUE

I have written about James Madison's important role in getting the U. S. Constitution ratified, and also in getting the original Bill of Rights through Congress. I also described how the first twelve amendment proposals included the ten amendments that came to be known as the Bill of Rights, and two others that were not ratified at that time, that is, by 1791. One of the two others was eventually ratified, in 1992. It became the 27th, and most recent, amendment, which provides: "No law, varying the compensation for the services of the Senators and Representatives, shall take effect, until an election of Representatives shall have intervened." Six States ratified this proposed amendment by the end of 1791, but that wasn't enough then, and as time passed and more States joined the U. S. A., it took more States to ratify. No deadline for ratification had been included, however, so the congressional salary amendment just sat there, waiting. By 1978, two more States had ratified. In 1982, however, an undergraduate college student wrote a term paper about the forgotten amendment proposal. His instructor scoffed at the student's idea that the proposed amendment could yet be ratified. The student, Gregory D. Watson, a 20-year-old sophomore at the University of Texas, Austin, accepted the challenge and began writing letters to the Legislatures of the States, urging them to vote to ratify the old amendment proposal, and one by one, they did! Between 1983 and 1992, 33 States voted to ratify. On May18, 1992, the National Archivist certified the ratification of what was now the 27th Amendment to the United States Constitution. And the votes kept coming in, so that by now, 45 of the 50 States have ratified the 27th Amendment, originated in Madison's time and with his efforts, ratified more than two centuries later, thanks to the determination of a young man named Gregory Watson, obviously an inspiration to my own efforts to bring about the reform and modernization of the United States Constitution.

P. D. L.